THE

ANTHOLOGY OF POEMS
COLLECTED AND COMPILED
FOR
THE BURMA STAR
ASSOCIATION

by

THE BOSTON AND NORTH CAMBRIDGESHIRE BRANCH

19 90

RICHARD KAY
80 Sleaford Road • BOSTON • Lincs • PE21 8EU

© Burma Star Association

British Library Cataloguing in Publication Data
The Stars : anthology of poems.
  I. Burma Star Association, *Boston and North
  Cambridgeshire Branch*
  821.91408

  ISBN 0 – 902662 – 97 – X
  ISBN 0 – 902662 – 98 – 8 pbk

Set in Bookman type on an AppleMac computer using a DTP publishing package as supplied by Gestetner Ltd. Camera ready copy printed by means of a Laser-Writer Plus printer.

Printed by
The Echo Press • 25 Swan Street • Loughborough •
Leicestershire • LE11 0BT

CONTENTS

POETRY

PUBLISHER'S PREFACE

These poems are a commemoration of the men and women of the Allied nations who served in the Burmese theatre of war between 1939 and 1945 – not only in the armed forces – and of those who waited at home for them. The verses have been collected by members of the Burma Star Association and some have previously been published in Regimental journals or in *Dekho* the journal of the Burma Star Association itself.

Much of this collection was written in Burma, some by prisoners of war in POW camps; some in the field of battle immediately before or after actual conflict; a few pieces have been written long after by those who returned and a few by relatives of those involved. Few men who returned came back without deep and lasting scars – in many instances seemingly deeper and more lasting than those acquired in other theatres of war. That all did not return is now, in many cases, no more than recorded fact. Those to whom it has meant so much more than mere recorded fact are now, perhaps daily, diminishing in numbers. To publish this collection of poetry, verse, even doggerel, whilst there are still those who do remember is perhaps an act of homage to those who did suffer in the conflict and to those who gave their fathers, brothers, sons. Some made the sacrifice voluntarily, many had no choice and, in any case, regarded it simply as their duty. It may seem to those who do not remember – and few below the age of sixty can have any very clear recollection – simply old soldiers recalling their past glories: but it is not just, nor even mainly, glory that is recalled and recorded. It is something that gave to those directly involved an awareness of values that today seem often to have been lost and to be at risk of being forgotten or even derided. These lines have been written almost exclusively by men and women who were, often very directly, involved in the desperately distressing struggle or, in a few instances, simply in the consequences of that struggle.

Just as Agincourt, Trafalgar, Waterloo, and even Mafeking and the Somme, are history so are the achievements – and the failures – of the 14th Army, and those forces who supported them, becoming history. But let it not be a history that merely records the great achieve-ments without recording the feel, the smell, even the taste of the jungle and the disgusting conditions that were endured, the appalling distress that was occasioned, the fear and the courage despite the fear, the gallantry and the inhumanity of men under stress and under orders. The men of the Burma Star Association are proud of what they did achieve – it would be strange if they were not – but they are not recorded here for those achievements to be emulated but rather so that they can be avoided for ever in the future.

Poetry is emotive – it is meant to be emotive: much of this poetry was written at times of great emotion and some of that is conveyed despite, or even sometimes perhaps because, of the shortcomings of the verses as formal poetry.

Many of these poets were poets only because they felt the urgent need to express, in some medium or other, feelings and thoughts that they had never previously experienced. They only knew that they needed to share their deepest feelings and that they needed to give something to others whilst they could do so – perhaps as a justification to themselves for their own actions.

Although poetry is the oldest art form in language and is crafted and honed by scholars and by both men and women of maturity and experience, it is also the vehicle often used by the young to try to express the developing emotions of the maturing years. It may not always be elegant but it is usually honest and sometimes eloquent because of its 'defects' rather than despite them.

Editing these lines has been difficult. The origins of some of the verses are unknown, others, although the authors are known, are posthumous. The temptation to amend, even rewrite, some of the lines has been great. In some minor instances this has been done but only if the editing has seemed to enhance the author's words – not to correct them.

Some of the authors have not been members of the Burma Star Association and some never could have been. Some of the verses come from wives, mothers, or others who were emotionally perhaps as deeply involved as those in the jungle. All these authors have been touched by the conflict, now so nearly forgotten, that was not quite like any other war in which Britain has been involved. It was, to the rest of the world, almost an aside – not quite a part of the war that everyone else was fighting. But to those involved it was for a time – and for some a very long time – their whole existence. Korea and Vietnam were, in their time, in the centre of the world stage. The Burma zone, except for brief periods such as at the time of the fall of Singapore, was never centre stage although at times its significance was enormous.

These pages record the emotions of some of those involved. There may be no Macaulay, no Siegfried Sassoon, nor even a Rupert Brooke represented here but collectively there is a great sense of comradeship and sacrifice and even that outmoded sentiment Patriotism. This is the poetry of that time, wry, awkward, unpolished though it sometimes is. So was Burma: and there is not always time to polish words when one is about to die.

We have tried to do justice to the men and women who wrote these words and those for whom they were written. May there never again be occasion to call for such verses.

FOREWORD

Many years ago the idea of compiling an anthology of poems written by men of Burma was discussed by two or three members of the 'PINWE CLUB', the battalion welfare organisation, whose members mainly served with the 9th. Battalion The Royal Sussex Regiment, with the 36th British Division in the Arakan of Burma, and then alongside the Americans and Chinese in North Burma (CBI).

Due to a prior commitment to publish the history of the battalion in World War II, it was deferred. However, following many requests from members, and some members of the general public, to compile a book of these works, and many are quite classics, I offered to take up the challenge and am more than pleased to be associated with the venture, for I served with the unit most of it's life.

I realised long ago that there was a great need for someone to compile an anthology of poems written by men and women of Burma, and their wives, of their feelings and experiences in those traumatic times. Also, those of our less fortunate comrades who were taken prisoner and who were subjected to barbaric treatment at the hands of the Japanese Militia.

Reading many of these works will bring a lump in the throat, and a tear to the eye, for they all tell a story based on facts, and reflect the attitudes of life under pressure, and the reflections of men and women who were caught up in it, and some written years after the end of hostilities.

Without compiling this anthology most of these poems would be lost for ever, and by undertaking the compilation of this book we are able to leave a tribute for posterity to those gallant men and women who fought and died for their country, in Burma and adjacent territories, for the peace we all love, however fragile it may be.

SANDY WILLIAMS

Acnowledgements

It is with great pride and satisfaction that I extend my thanks to all those people who have given permission to use their poems and those of their loved ones in this anthology and for the other material used in this book.

Because of the nature of this work it was never our intention to list the large number of contributors to this anthology of poems, the unique brotherhood of the Burma Star Association does not demand such recognition. Each author's name has been identified wherever known and the year, but some wished to be anonymous. During the selection of the poems sent we had to be positive and set a standard, anything with a political bias we chose not to print however good it was. Also, some provided were of a trivial nature and had no direct bearing on the main reason for undertaking the anthology, and as we had no shortage of material we were able to provide what we feel is to be an acceptable compostion.

Permission was obtained in the first instance from BSA HQ Officers and an open letter of intent dispatched to all BSA Branch Secretaries and the deadline date for objections declared. Now that that date has long since passed we are happy to proceed with the printing of this tribute to the Men and Women of Burma.

Again very many thanks to all who have provided the material in print and especially to the 'Pinwe Club' who provided approximately half of the total material used.

H. E. WILLIAMS (Ex 9th RSxR)

DISTRIBUTION OF SALES PROFITS

It has been agreed that the following will benefit from the profits from the book sales: –

The Burma Star Association General Fund	50% of the profit
The Boston & North Cambridgeshire Branch (who gave the project financial support)	30% of the profit
The Pinwe Club (for their support and commitment)	20% of the profit

---

When you go home, tell them of us and say:
"For your tomorrow, we gave our today."

WHY WEAR A POPPY?

"Please wear a Poppy," the lady said,
    And held one forth, but I shook my head.
Then I stopped and watched as she offered them
                                    there,
    And her face was old and lined with care,
But beneath the scars the years had made
    There remained a smile that refused to fade.

A boy came whistling down the street,
    Bouncing along on carefree feet.
His smile was full of joy and fun,
    "Lady," he said, "May I have one?"
When she'd pinned it on he turned to say,
    "Why do we wear a Poppy today?"

The lady smiled in her wistful way
    And answered, "This is Remembrance Day",
And the poppy there is the symbol for
    The gallant men who died in war;
And because they died, you and I are free,
    That's why we wear a poppy you see.

"I had a boy about your size,
    With golden hair and big blue eyes,
He loved to play and jump and shout,
    Free as a bird he would race about.
As the years went by he learned and grew
    And became a man as you will too."

"He was fine and strong, with a boyish smile,
    But he seemed to be with us such a little while.
When war broke out he went away;
    I still remember his face that day,
When he smiled at me and said, 'Goodbye,
    I'll be back soon, Mum, so please don't cry.'

"But the war went on and he had to stay,
   And all I could do was to wait and pray.
His letters told of the awful fight
   (I see it still in my dreams at night),
With the tanks and the guns, and the cruel barbed
                                         wire,
   And the mines and the bullets, and the bombs
                                     and fire.

Til at last, at last, the war was won –
   So that's why we wear a poppy, son."
The small boy turned as if to go,
   Then said: "Thanks, lady, I'm glad to know.
That sure did sound an awful fight,
   But, your son, did he come back alright?"

A tear rolled down the faded cheek;
   She shook her head, but did not speak.
I slunk away feeling sick with shame,
   And if you'd been me you'd have done the same.
For our thanks, in giving, are oft delayed,
   Though our freedom was bought – and
                              thousands paid.

And so when you see a poppy worn
   Try to think of the burden borne
By those, who gave their very all
   When asked to respond to their country's call;
That we at home in peace might live.
   So, wear a poppy; Remember, and Give!

Don Crawford

*(With thanks and compliments to the South West
London Branch)*

3.

The 'Shiny Ninth'

Fifty years ago, my lads, we marched along with pride,
  'Twas with the 'Shiny Ninth' and let no man e'er deride;
The 'Spit and Polish' soldiering and all those timely drills,
  Made us feel ten feet tall, without those age old frills.
For we were clad in battle dress of khaki-serge at that,
  With creases bold and brasses bright and a cap-badge
                                               in our hat:
We out-shone all the others, that's what we used to say,
  And ". . . second only to the 'Guards'. . ." was what we
                                             heard folks say.
Yes! we the 'Ninth of Sussex' were disciplined as well,
  And when we went to Burma we gave Jap merry hell;
Although the 'shine' of barrack life was left at India base,
  Our job was very clear indeed – the Jap from Burma
                                                  chase.
For now we speak of medals won, and great deeds done,
  We can look back with pride and thank God for the
                                            peace we've won.

'Sandy' H. E. Williams
Ex-Sgt. 9th Royal Sussex Regimen

The Thoughts and Prayers of an Army Mule

Please be kind to me, Old Soldier, now that we're both on
  line of march; I try so hard to please you!

Please also remember, it's NOT ALWAYS MY FAULT when
  my load slips – for sometimes my girth straps are
                not fastened properly, by you know who!

Please remember never overload me – but always keep

4.

within my limitations – to let me please you!

Please feed me and water me and look me over every day for
problems – since I cannot tell you when I'm in pain –
yet I also suffer too!

Please note that I also remember happier times back at
Base HQ, and I certainly NEVER asked your
veterinary people to de-vocalise me, either!

Please bring me to a quick end – should I be wounded badly
– so that I shall then die honourably – as a good
soldier!

My understanding is that your Jesus Christ was born in a
stable – and a stable is my own spiritual home too!
Perchance therein lies the affinity and comradeship
between Man and Mule!

In writing these words for me, my old mule-walla Sahib
honours his promise – and honours me by signing
his name! Barra Salaams!

Signed as promised.
Frank Turner, Major, III Brigade, Chindits

ODE TO A BEARER

Oh, faithful bearer,
Who heals my woes!
Oh, constant wearer,
Of all my clothes!
Oh fount of virtue!
Oh, form of Grace!
It wouldn't hurt you
To wash your face!

Unknown
Taken from a SEAC

5.

'DAWN'

Dawn on the Mayo Range
    Is always new and beautiful and strange,
To you; Because the night before
    You're never absolutely sure
The day just past
    Was not your last.
And so the early golden ray
    That brings you yet another day
Evokes a silent grateful prayer,
    It's nice to find that you're still there.

Cyril Grimes, Ex-Sgt
9th Bn The Royal Sussex Regt.

THE LETTER
(Mandalay Hill)

Grotesquely spilled and disarrayed they lie,
    Like broken dolls abandoned after play,
Their empty eyes stare coldly to the sky,
    To everlasting night and endless day.

The dolls that yesterday were men,
    With yearning wistful dreams of those held dear,
Still linked by stilted phrases from a pen
    That bridged the world and brought them
                              warmly near.

A Letter moulding in a pack
    Pleads "Please, oh please, oh please come back",
But in this godforsaken place
    Dogs rip and tear and eat his face.

Gordon Nimse

6.

Brave Pilgrimage

(A Tribute to the 1st Gloucesters, 1942)

By swamp and tangled jungle way,
From Rangoon on to Mandalay!
Day after day, week after week,
By thorny path and poisoned creek;
On, where there is no path at all,
Where it is death to fail or fall,
Where sun, soil, insect, beast and snake,
Their toll of every traveller take;
Where fever lurks in every breath,
And every yard is walked with Death;
The venomed and forbidden way
From Rangoon on to Mandalay.

This is the route the Gloucesters went,
Our own, our glorious Regiment;
When every bog, and bush, and tree
Gave cover to an enemy.
Unfed, outnumbered, and worn out,
Yet with the strength to turn about
And charge the overwhelming foe,
And turn again, and onward go
Along the muddy, bloody way
From Rangoon on to Mandalay.

For two long months, by day and night
They fought, marched, turned again
to fight!
Their dead they must leave where they stay
Along the road to Mandalay.
March! Halt! Turn! Charge! Did Glory's page
E'er hold a braver pilgrimage?
Mark it in gold on Honours' Scroll,

And with just pride of race extoll
These, who their lives for England spent,
    Our own, our glorious Regiment.
Add Letpadan and Paungde
    To Alexandria long ago,
And all the other honours won
    Since their proud history was begun.

These men did all that any might
    All stress and strain that men may know
They fought and conquered, plus the foe!
    And Letpadan and Paungde
Stand out in their special fame,
    Because here was a place to name!
'Gainst Burman dacoit, and cruel Jap,
    'Gainst natural peril and mishap
They battled on, and justified
    The Back Badge emblem of their pride,
Making each day a 'Crispin's Day'
    On the dread road to Mandalay.

Honour the living! For the dead
    Let no unhappy tear be shed;
They fought and fell as brave men should
    For England, and the common good.
Pray God that we our part may play,
    Like those who stay 'til 'Judgement Day'
Along the road to Mandalay.

H A Dawson.

(This poem has been published in "The Back Badge", the journal of the Gloucestershire Regiment, and is produced by kind permission of the editor, Lt. Col. H.L.T. Radice, MBE)

How '60' Went to Burma

When the powers that be at Simla
 Were sitting round one day,
A bigwig mentioned Burma
 And the road to Mandalay.
Another mentioned 'Sixty'
 Doing nothing at Lahore
And said "Let's send them out there
 For they've never been before."

Imagine '60's panic when, one
 Smiling Sunday morn,
The 'genhounds', spread around the news
 Of movements yet unborn.
As '60' started packing, filling up,
 And guessing where
They'd all end up eventually, and if
 They'd all get there.

Just where the destination was to be
 Was very hard to say.
Was it invasion of 'Aul Oirelan' or
 The road to Mandalay.
In any case 'Old Sixty' – they got
 Ready just the same,
Prepared to go to Timbuctoo or
 Just to play the game.

The 'gen' came out 'twas Singapore
 The Squadron had to go.
And more than one observing man
 Exclaimed "I told you so!"
Then '60' bid a fond farewell
 To India's coral strand,
And off they set to Singapore
 As to a promised land.

The Thirteenth day of February
   Nineteen Forty-One
Saw thirteen planes of '60'
   Setting eastwards in the sun.
By night they all made Dum Dum
   And quite early next day
They all set out for Rangoon – an'
   The road to Mandalay

They all got there – no matter how
   As Sixty always will,
That night they were in Maxims'
   Honky Tonk and Silver Grill.
The folk all took them to their heart
   And said: "Come here to stay
We'd like to have you with us –
   On the road to Mandalay."

This poem was written by –
   Sgt *Johnny Johnson*, 60 Sqn RAF
   Who was killed in the Malayan retreat.

Note:
   *The original orders were to go to Singapore but were countermanded. The majority of the groundcrews and admin' staff went to Calcutta, and by ship (the **SS EKMA**) to Singapore. They did not leave the ship except for pleasure visits into the city. After a couple of days or so the ship sailed back to the Port of Rangoon in Burma and joined up with the Aircrews at Migladon on 12 March 1941. The living quarters were not completed, so they were all billeted in a large Army camp adjacent to the airfield. Mingladon was a fairly large civilian airfield in those days and was considered the main airfield between India and Singapore.*

FROM MALAYA (KUNTAN) TO SINGAPORE. TO BURMA, TO INDIA (LAHORE)

We came from North Malaya
    To the shores of Singapore
By leaps and bounds and lorry rides
    As never known before.

The little Jap was on our tail
    With bombs and cannon shell
We had no means of stopping him
    So we ran like ruddy hell.

Our staple food was Bully Beef
    With biscuits hard as rock –
Inside a week the best of us
    Were fit to be in dock.

Every day at crack of dawn
    We had to do PIs
With one eye cast upon our job
    The other on the skies.

As sure as fate at half past nine
    We'd hear the sirens' howls –
By gosh, it tore your very soul –
    'Twas tied up in your bowels.

Oh, how we ran those red hot days
    We raced with one another
We died a score of ruddy deaths
    In that mad rush for cover.

We never had a sec' to spare
    As in the trench we lay,
We'd hear the drone of Tojo's kites,
    Perhaps our turn today.

Then one of us would see them
    – The silver sons of Hell –
But where they'd drop their load of death
    Not one of us could tell.

With fearful eyes we'd watch them
    – In twenty-sevens they flew –
Close packed in tight formation
    Against the skies of blue.

Right overhead we'd hear them roar
    And then that awful sound
Of pear-shaped bombs on way to earth
    The shriek of Bask'ville's hounds.

The earth was torn with jagged holes
    The shrap' flew far and wide.
The very trenches heave and twist
    Shaking the chaps inside.

We hear the cry 'they're here again'
    And how we want to run,
We hear the sound of diving planes
    The rattle of their gun.

The bullets sizzle by our trench,
    We hear the Bofors chatter,
The cannon shells set kites alight
    As in them they do splatter.

What would we do without those boys,
  Who man the Bofors guns,
They make the bombing far from fun
  For Nippon's airmen sons.

Thick oily smoke curls upwards,
  A petrol dump again,
We cannot hope for them to miss
  When dropping bombs like rain.

The aircraft that I worked on
  Is blazing like a pyre
Thirty-thousand pounds worth
  Like a Guy Fawkes fire.

They sent us things as bad as bombs
  'Cos they were live and kicking.
Little blokes on ends of 'chutes
  Fair meat for our picking.

We pelted them with shrapnel
  They got it in the neck,
Half the swine were very dead
  Before they hit the deck.

Now India has claimed us
  The land of sun and grit.
God help us if we have to fight
  'Cos we aint ruddy fit.

> **Author unknown**
> Written about May '42
> And identified with '60' Squadron.

'60' Squadron
Return from Burma 1942

'60' Squadron at Lahore, the year is '42,
  The number's the same one, but all the rest is new.
There are only ghosts and shadows, faint echoes, little sign
  Of the '60' at Umbala in 1939.

Reunion dinner at Lahore is just a fleeting wave,
  The real reunion we would know is had beyond the grave.
Forgive us, you who come now, if we forbear to cheer;
  It's not a want of welcome but in our hearts a tear
For those who were old '60' and cannot now be here.

In the crewroom back at Mingladon when we were
                        feeling low
  We'd seek out Johnny Johnson and from him then
                        would flow
A constant stream of sparkling wit
  'Til we'd forget our Burma life – the ennui of it.

Air Observer Smudger Smith, another cheerful bloke
  Who always had a laugh at life, who always had a joke.
His little black moustache, his grin, his Fleet Air Arm walk.
  What do they know of '60', the new ones as they talk.

Do you remember Robert, Henry, Joseph, Lofty Pile?
  A man with muscles like a mule, a heart devoid of guile.
Simple and true and brave and fine, from Canada he came
  And yet they speak of '60' as if it were the same.

Do you remember Biffy? Just a kid – too young to die.
  Nobbie Clark and Ossie Webb whose death made
                        Curly cry.
Curly Fowler died next day, Ace Gregory and the rest,
  Connie Connell, Dobson, all the bravest and the best.

Paddy Westrop Bennet who in the tropic's glare
  Would dream about the chicken farm he wanted
                                                back in Eire.
The Terror of the Tori Khel we used to call him then
  And now he's gone, one more we'll never see again.

Charlie Gill and Cocker Logan, Kingswell Bowden too.
  Baby Bowden is a prisoner if Tokyo news is true.
Jimmy Appleton, it seems, was drowned off Singapore.
  All of those were '60' that we shall see no more.
So '60' Squadron passes, all this is something new.
  God call us by another name in 1942.

Sgt *John Peel* of '60' Sqdn
Composed on the retreat from Burma, when most of '60'
were killed.

60 SQUADRON
A REPLY TO SERGEANT JOHN PEEL

We came to fill in '42
  The gaps that war had left
We found a welcome, sad but true
  From those of friends bereft.

We came and filled in '42
  The ranks of those left thin.
We had, at home, some suffered too,
  But come we did to win.

The ranks we filled in '42
  Once more became alive.
We drank the pride and purpose too
  And felt ourselves revive.

15.

Our '60' Squadron had become
    Once more a Unit proud
To bear the number, far from home
    That stood above the crowd.

We learned so fast in '42
    We held our heads erect,
We had good comrades, veterans too,
    We had the will, no flaws detect.

The aircraft came, in '42
    With aircrews fresh and hard.
We stood dismayed – they were not new
    But salvaged from scrapyard.

We did our best in '42
    To make our aircraft sound,
We had no spares, just will to do
    The best that could be found.

Our Squadron went, in '42
    To face the foe once more,
We were the first, the best renew
    That left from safe Lahore.

We went to Bengal, and there pursue
    Once more to take up arms,
We welded well, we old and new
    And found our fame spread fast.

First to Asonsol, there uphold
    The heritage '60' had,
We proved our worth, us new and old
    And in our hearts were glad.

We stood our ground in '42
　　'Til all our kites were done.
Bomb and strafing failed to do
　　What had transpired in '41.

We watched you leave, you old ones
　　And saw replacements come,
Your tour of duty over,
　　You left us to go home.

We moulded well, we new ones
　　With newer ones arrive,
We found ourselves the old ones
　　And kept the Squadron live.

We did quite well, we new ones
　　That seemed all at sea before,
We stood the test, as old ones
　　Had done in days of yore.

Through years of toil and battlecry
　　That ghosts of '60' gone,
Had borne with heads held ever high
　　Our Squadron proud had come.

We did the job in '45
　　That '42 demanded
We, new ones, older now but live
　　To deeds as war commanded.

I like to think in later years,
　　That '60' lives for ever.
I know that in my heart appears
　　A pride time cannot sever.

I see the ghosts of those gone by
    That served our famous number.
Each in their own part did but try,
    As war demands encumber.

The Squadron proud, reborn again
    Still holds it's Standard high,
We, of the old, pray it retains
    The spirit known in years gone by.

We're proud of you the new ones
    That joined the Squadron old.
We are beside you in our hearts
    For, we know, yours are gold.

H. E. Parsons,
'60' Squadron1942 to 1945

A BRAVE MAN

Never was he ever bored,
    What memories he has stored,
Of those wartime bygone years,
    Remembering brings him near to tears.
Memories of battles past
    Still linger in his mind;
His youth had passed so fast
    And never again to find,
His youth was spent in jungles green,
    To fight for England was his aim;
The toil, the fear, made him so keen
    For victory, without fame.

D. E. C.

Via SINGAPORE

We've got a blinkin' Zoo here,
    But it ain't in Regents' Park;
They never sweep the roads here,
    And the jungle's pretty dark;
We've muck up to our eyes here,
    And the town ain't on the map,
A stick can be a snake here,
    And a tree may be a Jap.

It's hard tack and 'compo rations'.
    Dirty bilge and bully beef;
There's no time for steak and onions,
    When a Jap's behind a leaf.
But, by heck! through swamp and mangrove
    We shall settle this old score;
We're coming back to England –
    And that's via Singapore!

Author unknown

IN MEMORIAM

By the road and the hills lie the scattered seed,
    A bamboo cross on each lonely grave,
Shimmering silence and jungle weed
    Enfold and touch lightly — here sleep the brave.

Not yet the fruit of your dying be tasted,
    The sun and the rain, no harvest unfold;
But rest, we shall see that the seed was not wasted,
    The living remember, the tale shall be told.

Cyril Grimes
Sgt. 9th Royal Sussex Regt: 36 Div.

MEDALS

Go and pin your medals on,
    Be proud they're yours to wear,
Pull your shoulders back a bit
    And let the youngsters stare.
They are yours by right of war
    By service to the Crown,
They are symbols that you
    Never let your country down.
Wear them proudly on your chest
    And let who will deride
They are yours by right of war;
    So carry them with pride.

Desmond Burgess.

A TRIBUTE

There's a river called the Chinwin
                flowing swiftly through the night
  And a railway that is bloodstained
                  by the slaves who lost the fight,
There are serried ranks of tombstones
                shielding men from near and far
  And shining o'er the peaceful scene,
                  a lonely Burma Star.

E. Kemsley

RICE

We hear of great victories won in the West
    And dream of release and those we love best,
We swallow with joy most incredible tales
    And it's hardly a wonder we got off the rails,
All illusions are shattered in less than a trice
    When somebody mentions that bloody word - RICE.

We scramble in muck heaps for brushes and pails,
    Our life is an ill-fated scramble for nails,
Our senior officers wrangle in vain
    With the Nips who have nothing to show but disdain,
But no matter how heavily loaded the dice
    The fruit of defeat is undoubtedly – RICE.

We seize what we can every day through the wire
    And the troops get the best from the 'ladies for hire',
'Tis a rare sight indeed to see live Brigadiers
    Grabbing buns through the bars like Regents Park
                                  bears.
But such gluttony cannot be labelled a vice
    When we know that the only alternative's - RICE.

Some Colonels and Majors and Subalterns too
    Reverse the procedure we've seen at the zoo,
And some live on memories prior to the blitz
    Of epicurean repasts held at the Ritz.
But whether our manners are nasty or nice
    It's a quid to a farthing – the answer is – RICE.

We've no blankets, nor clothes and we sleep on the floor,
  We have scarcely a window to close and no door,
And a problem most weighty for someone to solve
  Is how to maintain some hygienic resolve.
But who gives a hoot for the menace of lice
  As long as those Japs keep giving us – RICE.

J. F. McGregor

Written March 1942 at Shamshuipo POW Camp
by Lt J. F. McGregor, ADC to GOC

THE 14TH ARMY

Men say the echoes that the gun-fire woke
  Round Pelu Peaks and Pegu, sleep once more,
And by that weary Irrawaddy shore
  Only the fishermen send up their smoke;
Far-seen and lonely on the silent stream,
  Where death was once the substance, life the dream.

The stir and rumour of ten thousand men
  Moved in those forests once, and shook the leaves,
Sudden and secret as the hot wind breathes,
  Tossing the jungle, and is still again;
Silence has taken all; the runways fade,
  The jungle marches where our camps were made.

Beneath the monsoon cloud-wrack and the rain,
  The steaming valleys of the Kabaw sleep,
And all the jungles of the Chindwin keep,
  Their savage silence rendered back again.

Steven Bracher

HOME FROM THE SEA

A TRIBUTE TO LORD LOUIS MOUNTBATTEN

Home to Romsey, home to rest,
    Home to the folk who knew him best,
Dignitaries and farm hands too,
    With a sob in their voice, they spoke of you.
Far-flung empires their messages sent
    To Viceroy so high, so eminent;
Queens and princes bowed their heads
    For the loss of advisor, uncle and friend.
The riderless, jet black horse
    With his riding boots reversed in course.
A man among men, who lived to serve,
    Warm and friendly, but steely of nerve.
Killed at sea, but not in battle,
    No boom of enemy guns a rattled;
Oh! senseless crime, what have they gained?
    They shall not further their cause this way,
We dare not judge, we dare not say,
    Only ask – has another man died in vain?
Unto the haven where he would be,
    Safe from alarm, but facing the sea
To listen in peace to the ocean's drone.
    This man for all seasons, is going home,
Home to Romsey, home from the sea,
    Goodnight Lord Louis, peace be with thee.

Phyl Stiles

GOD'S IN HIS HEAVEN
(The Irrawaddy Crossing)

With cold indifferent hate the guns have sown
    Their instant flowering seeds of acrid dust,

Black towering weeds whose searing stamens moan
    For obscene consummation of their lust;

And those they pierced and rent beyond recall
    Knew pain transcending e'en their prior dread,

And God (who sees each tiny sparrow fall)
    Notes that a further hundred men are dead.

Gordon Nimse

TO MY SON

I think that all is quiet where you are lying,
    The smoke and dust of battle long since gone,
Now little birds and shy small animals come freely
    About their daily life, while you sleep on.
When the light of day touches the hilltop,
    Folding away the mist that evening laid
With careful hands to shield you from the darkness,
    That you might rest there safe and unafraid;
One shining ray will light where you are lying,
    Spreading its radiance like a flag unfurled,
A memory of the glory of your passing,
    And of the courage that you gave the world.

Anonymous (Mother)

ODE TO ENGLAND
(from)
Stanley Prisoner of War Camp – 1942

My England, My England,

How well you've stood the test
    Of death rained on you from the skies,
By Huns like fiends possessed,
    But England never dies.

When last I saw you, beauty slept
    O'er your fair land serene,
The scourge of war had not yet crept
    To wake you from your dream.

How much you've suffered time will tell
    When these dark days are past,
And right prevails, to sound the knell
    Of him whose die is cast.

When challenged and stood forth to fight
    With allies, had you known,
Would leave you 'gainst the foes great might
    To carry on alone.

You did not falter England brave
    Your pledges you would keep,
From tyranny the world to save
    'tho' traitors chose to sleep.

New enemies were in the field,
    Their time to strike was near,
When they thought that you would yield,
    Their imprecations fear.

Now came against you from Japan
    Vast hordes, like beasts of prey,
Your colonies they over-ran
    Hong Kong down to Malay.

Interned, impotent, we out here
    Must wait, and pray, and smile
With courage and without fear,
    In this endurance vile.

With Sword of Justice in your hand,
    March on till victory's won,
And peace once more upon the land
    Of England soon shall come.

Then from your many scars arise
    Triumphant, proud, sublime,
And may you rest, your rule be wise
    Until the end of time.

Fred Kelly

TO RUBY 'IN ABSENTIA'
Stanley Prisoner of War Camp – 1942

Day by day I place a cross
    To mark the space of time
In bondage spent, Ah what a loss
    To those of me and mine.

The weary days are spent in thought
    Of one so dear to me,
Who waits I know, in patience fraught
    With dire uncertainty.

Do not despair my darling wife,
     The time is near on hand
When these sad years of war and strife
     Will end and peace will stand.

Tis just a year since you and I
     In Melbourne, days we spent,
Together, happy ne'er a sigh,
     In search of pleasure bent.

Tho' 'twas not all the joy we sought
     As many an hour we stayed,
In 'Fawker Mansions' wrapt in thought
     And for the future prayed.

Both you and I, we were quite sure
     That when the blow did fall,
That through the scourge of this great war,
     Our love would conquer all.

That I'd return to duty dear
     And leave you far away,
But this we knew, there was no fear,
     We'd meet again one day.

That day has yet to come my love,
     Though distant now it seems,
As I pray to Him above,
     To grant me all my dreams.

Eight short weeks, they soon passed by,
     Together all the time,
Long in my memory they will lie,
     As a monumental shrine.

Then on return my heart was sad,
No joy, just grief and pain,
When thinking of the days we'd had,
When will they come again?

E'er I left to sail away,
A letter to me you gave,
Of which I treasure, read each day,
My loneliness to save.

I close my eyes in constant strain,
To wonder how you are,
That God may bring about again,
My Ruby from afar.

Till then sweetheart I'll wait and pray,
God bless you, keep you well,
Speed on, speed on, that happy day,
When we've so much to tell.

Of all these days lived in the past,
In separation drear,
And hope that they will be the last,
That you'll be ever near.

Once more my darling little wife,
Au revoir and not goodbye,
God bring you safe through all this strife,
With me remain for aye.

Fred Kelly

A Tribute to the Officers and Men
OF
HMS Searcher
6 September 1945.

I have found new enchantment all this day,
    With hair wind-ruffled gazing out to sea,
Watching the silver flying-fishes play,
    Feeling as light as they, as careless, free.
Night brought fresh beauty, on the leaping foam
    A million fire-flecks mocked the starry sky,
I seemed to see the countless lights of home,
    So calm and tranquil shining brilliantly.
I felt a man again; gone was the past,
    With all its burden vanished far astern;
I'd found new friends and kindness, seen at last
    Our human fire-flecks gloriously burn.
In friendship firm, I see and, what is more,
    In peace as gallant as you were in war.

An ex-POW (Japan)

From one of many who used to be a drooping melancholy POW but now feels on top of the world. Thanks to you and the magic of the sea.

"BON VOYAGE".

ODE TO THE 14TH ARMY
DECEMBER 1944

They loved their Scottish homeland, and English scented lanes,
  They loved their great Welsh mountains and gentle
                                summer rains,
But now they sleep in Burma, where the river Chinwin flows,
  A small white cross above their heads, the names their
                                comrades knew.
They viewed their little village streets where lights did gleam
                                and glow,
  They loved the pictures and to dance with pretty girls
                                they knew,
They left their happy homeland, across the sea to die;
  Their youth a brief glory which sped so swiftly by:
Unfurl their flag of freedom; salute your gallant sons.
  They came from every walk of life to fire and man the guns;
And through the skies, across the seas, o'er many foreign lands,
  They met the tyrant enemy and smashed his heathen bands.
And when this war is over, and peace once more returns,
  We'll think of those we left behind as we watch our home
                                fires burn;
We'll think of all those gallant's neath Burma's sweating soil,
  Who made the supreme sacrifice, the Japanese to foil,
From Dimapur to Kohima, through Imphals bloody plain
  The battle raged for many months through heat and
                                monsoon rain;
By Tamu's steaming jungle, along the Tiddim Road
  And up the chocolate staircase the gallant way they strode.
They rode across the frontier into Mandalay.
  From Fort White into Tokyo; we know no other way;
And when the 'Rising Sun' is out for good the freedom flag will fly,
  Salute the Fourteenth Army lads, they weren't afraid to die.

Anonymous

A Little Mixed Up

Just a line to say I'm living, that I'm not among the dead;
  Though I'm getting more forgetful and more mixed up
                              in my head,
For, sometimes I can't remember when I stand at the foot
                              of the stair,
  If I must go up for something, Or I've just come down
                              from there,
And before the fridge so often, my poor mind is filled
                              with doubt,
  Have I just put some food away, or have I come to take
                              some out?
And there's times when it is dark out, with my night-cap
                              on my head,
  I don't know if I'm retiring, or just getting out of bed.
So, if it's my turn to write to you, there's no need
                              getting sore,
  I may think that I have written to you and don't want to
                              be a bore.
So, remember – I do love you, and wish that you were here;
  But now it's almost mail time, so I must say
                              "Goodbye dear".
P.S. There I stood beside the mail box with a face so
                              very red,
  Instead of mailing you my letter, I had opened it instead.

Anonymous

THE 36TH ROAD TO MANDALAY

With India and the Arakan behind us,
    The road to Mandalay did find us,
Fighting along the corridor from the North;
    Chaungs, rain and mud as we sallied forth,
From Mogaung, to Pinwe and Naba,
    Thence on for Christmas at Katha.
The tough fighting of Pinwe did leave us
    Looking for a Merry Christmas without fuss;
Short was our stay and our respite;
    For the Japs were preparing for a fight,
The ease in the capture of Mahlaingong,
    Was the reverse to the long struggle for Myitson,
Many fought hard and long, and some gave their all,
    In the dreadful struggle of this tough battle,
Was but a step on the long way –
    South, on the 'Road to Mandalay'.
So we of the 36th are pleased to say –
    We were proud to take part in the fight
                on the way to Mandalay.

Sandy H. E. Williams, Ex-Sgt
9th Royal Sussex Regiment.
36th British Division.

DEATH OF A SOLDIER

The jungle broods in silence, not a leaf is on the move,
  No birds to sing, no animals to roar,
All life has long departed from the ground, and
                          the trees above,
  Escaped from this mad, man-made, thing called war.

A sniper in the trees is giving trouble on the right,
  If you don't keep your head down, you'll get shot,
When you hear the bullet pass by, then you know that
                          you're alright,
  It's the soldier just behind who's had his lot.

When darkness falls, remove his tags, his paybook
                          and effects,
  Then wrap him in his blanket, feeling grim,
Just scrape a hole, and roll him in, a friend will then elect
  To say a short, sharp sermon, over him.

Scrape back the earth, erect a stake, to mark where
                          he is laid,
  And on it cut his number, rank and name,
You curse the war, the enemy, the sacrifice he made,
  Wondering what it's for, and who's to blame.

The battle's done, advance again, we leave him in the sun,
  Neath his marker, in the jungle, and who knows,
We wonder if they'll find him when the victory is won,
  And they're put in one large graveyard, all in rows.

We wonder if it's worth it, will this brave new world to be,
  Be what we want, or moonshine in the sky,
For freedom we are fighting, but with one thing I agree,
  But for the grace of God, man, there I lie.

                     Stan Chapman, Sgt. RAOC 33rd Corps
                     (Written at Shwebo)

2ND DIVISION'S RELIEF OF KOHIMA
Sung to the tune of Red River Valley

There's a place in the East called Kohima,
It's a place that we all know so well,
It was here that we lost all our manhood
And where most of our brave comrades fell.
We are proud of our second Division
And the great stand for freedom they made
And they swore in that place called Kohima
That the Jap domination would fade.

There are Scotsmen, Tommies, and Taffies,
And one flag we will fight to uphold,
And that flag will fly in Great Britain,
And it's stories will one day be told.

There's a place in the East called Kohima,
It's a place we all know so well,
And our comrades that lie in Kohima,
In the glory of Britain will dwell.

Anonymous

34.

To The Soldiers of Malaya

Heroically, you fought and died,
    In vain you strove to stem the tide
Of inexorably advancing foe,
    Alas, by what means could you know
Resistance was doomed to fail?
    For ere the first war trumpets' hail
Had sounded, it was so decreed
    That you, in England's hour of need
Should fall, and by falling, gain
    The time her armies to arrange
Afresh, that she might better face
    The onslaught of an alien race.
When England's final victory has been won,
England might kneel to you – her 'Sons'.

Anonymous

35.

A New Zealand Soldier's Prayer

Be with me God, the night is dark, the night is cold,
My little spark of courage dies,
The night is long, stay with me God and make
me strong.
I love a game, I love a fight,
I hate the dark, I love the light,
I love my child, I love my wife,
I am no coward I just like life.
I'm just a man my mother bore,
A simple man and nothing more,
But God of strength and gentleness,
Be pleased to make me nothing less.
I know that Death is just a door,
I know what we are fighting for -
'Place for the kids, our brothers freed,
A kinder world, a cleaner breed'.
Help me O God, when death is near,
To mock the haggard face of fear,
That when I fall, if fall I must,
My soul may triumph in the dust.

Anonymous New Zealander

The History of Two Div. in Burma

The 'Regiments' of Scotland, Wales, and English counties,
  Training on India's western boundaries,
Suddenly had a move to north-east Assam,
  The time had come for battle with the enemy from Japan.

Imphal was surrounded; Kohima lay under siege;
  Road links cut and the Jap doing as he pleased.
All haste to the railhead at Dimapur;
  In the distance the battleground, the hills and jungle
                                        of Manipur.

Nagpur, Calcutta, across Brahmaputra to the narrow
                                        gauge line.
  Big Slim's big worry will they get there in time?
Their task to relieve Kohima and open the road to Imphal.
  The door to India was wide open. They did not fail.

A brief sharp attack and the gallant Kohima garrison
                                        was relieved,
  For over two weeks they had been under a very
                                        bloody siege.
Richards' fifteen hundred had fought day and night,
  Thwarting the aims of Sato's thirty-first division's
                                        fanatical fight.

Pushed into an area a few hundred yards square,
  Trees smashed to pieces, the dead buried here and there,
First aid for the wounded in shallow unprotected pits,
  Alas, many suffering shell and mortar direct hits.

Kuki Picquet, Garrison Hill, FSD Ridge, were strong points
                                        by name,
  Each told a story, each had won fame.
With the garrison relieved, these positions the division took
                                        over,
  Under the command of a general by the name of Grover.

37.

Supplies came by air, beware the free drop,
  Every tree on Garrison Hill with a parachute on top.
Night after night the Japs did attack,
  It fell early to the Durhams to beat them back.

The Scots, Welsh, Berks, Norfolks, Worcesters, and LFs,
                              each had their show,
  None did it better than the Dorsets at the DC's bungalow,
Supported by gunners, sappers, medics, signals and
                              armour, second to none,
  The division finally routed the men of the rising sun.

Six weeks it had taken at terrible cost,
  There's a memorial at Kohima to those who were lost.
The chase is on, the Japs in full flight,
  They offer token resistance, they lack the will to fight.

The aim now is to link up with IV Corps at Imphal
  70 miles down the twisting Manipur Road, not much
                              better than a trail,
The gunners pounded the flanks, troops and armour
                              down the road,
  The monsoon had started but the advance never slowed.

The link-up came on June twenty second at milestone 108
  Japs were running fast and there had been a good killing
                              rate,
Round up the stragglers, then into tents just off the road
  Where we all watched the East Africans take over the load.
Calcutta, Bombay and Delhi, its leave at last without
                              monsoon,
  Reinforced and refreshed then on to Rangoon.

                    Written by a **2 Div Gunner** in Burma

A REMEMBRANCE POEM FOR V/J DAY

APPRAISAL

Let us stand and think a while, of those who gave their all,
Of those who fought and died for us, when they
answered the call.
Before that day in August, when Hostilities did cease,
They suffered untold agonies, to bring to us this peace.

Today we remember, that first V/J Day,
That took place in SEAC so far away.
To stand erect and let us bow our head,
And say a small prayer, for each of our dead.

Those of the Navy, and Army, as well
And those of the Air Force, who saved us from hell.
Let us remember that they gave their all
They readily answered, when they heard the call.

From all walks of life, came those warriors we knew,
Who donned their uniforms, of khaki or blue.
They'd heard the call, that on trumpets was blown,
And they answered that call, from both factory
and home.

They went overseas, midst the clapping and cheers,
They hadn't much thought for worries or fears.
Just one thought in mind, for Freedom they'd fight.
To live as free men as once was their right.

So think of these men, and womenfolk too,
Who answered the call, when the Great Trumpet blew.
In Burma, Malaya and Java, they fought.
To win victory, was their only thought.

Bravely they struggled, bravely they died,
  To give us the Freedom, on which we relied.
Now in each of these countries, where they fought and fell,
  Stands an obelisk of stone, with a story to tell.

Of unsung heroes, who died not in vain,
  And also for others, who still live 'in pain'.
Remember those heroes, remember and pray,
  FOR ALL YOUR TOMORROWS, THEY GAVE THEIR
                                    TODAY.
                              Author not known

'FORTY-ONE YEARS AFTER' REUNION

Tonight we meet from near and far
  In comradeship of the Burma Star;
Tonight once more our minds will
  Turn to the memories of Uncle Bill,
To memories of steaming heat,
  Of jungle trails and aching feet.
What days of tribulations those,
  Pursuing ruthless hidden foes!
A cunning game, a campaign to be won
  Beneath the blazing Burmese sun.
The neutral jungle gave no ease
  To the Fourteenth Army or to Japanese
And we recall that life was grim
  But this was shared by General Slim.
We were a 'brotherhood' indeed
  Of whom one day the world would read;
A band of men a cause well serving
  To fight for something worth preserving.
The words are those of General Slim –
  Saturday night we remembered him.

Written after the Burma Star Reunion '87

These verses have no title but are headed:
'I've a tale to tell of a job done well'

When you grow old
    And your heart grows cold
And the hairs on your head are few
    You can look back on life
Midst the Burma strife
    And tell a tale or two.

So buy me a beer
    Bring me a chair
And a tale I'll tell to you
    Of the famous 19th Dagger Div
And the job they did so well
    They called them India's Home Guard
But they knew there would come a day
    When they showed the world their mettle
On the road to Mandalay.

The Sikhs, Baluch, Raj, Rif
    and Johnny Gurkha too
The Welsh, Berks and Worcesters
    Have showed their colours true
Across the Irrawady was their
    Tough route to crack
It was hell it was bloody But they drove the
devils back
    Yes they drove the yellow devils
From Rangoon to Mandalay, and when they took
Fort Dufferin
    It was their greatest day.

The wireless screamed their
    Victory of fall of Mandalay
But only those that fought there
    Knew the price they had to pay.
So now that war is over,
    And peace has come to stay,
Remember those that fought and fell
    On the road to Mandalay.

W A Price

THE PADRE

The Padre's got a cushy job, he roams about all day,
    He doesn't work, he merely talks and wastes his time
                                         away.
He wears his collar back to front, and looks professional
    But don't you let him take you in, he doesn't work at all.

It's War boys, and we've got to fight, and that's our job for
                                       now;
    The CO and the officers are here to tell us how,
The MO's here to patch us up – we'll need him in this war –
    But is there anybody who knows what a Padre's for?

The Army must be mechanised if we're to make a show
    And every Fusilier admits we want an MTO.
A Quartermaster there must be to superintend the store,
    But only the Almighty knows just what the Padre's for.

42.

And yet I've just been thinking, chaps, that surely he was
                                                    sent
    To do a job of some kind, for he's not an ornament;
I've heard it said, by friends of mine who met a few in
                                                    France,
    That Padres can come up to scratch if men give them a
                                                    chance.

I get my problems and my thoughts, I get temptations, too,
    And secret fears I'd like to share with someone, Bill,
                                                    don't you?
We're not the only ones like that, there must be many more,
    And so I've sometimes wondered if that's what a Padre's
                                                    for.

Mind you, I'm not afraid to die, and I don't ask for fuss,
    But we've got girls or wives and kids who think the
                                                    world of us
And if I get knocked out tonight and laid I know not where,
    Although I'm not a churchy chap I wouldn't mind
                                                    a prayer.

Take that young fellow over there who's getting on so well –
    If he gets shot his mother's heart is going to ache
                                                    like hell;
If Padre wrote it couldn't bring him back, for nothing could,
    And yet she'd be relieved to know that someone
                                                    understood.

That someone understood, you know, someone who was
                                                    nearby,
    Who lived with him, and knew his name, perhaps who
                                                    saw him die.
And every mother in the hour of bitterness and loss
    Might like to know that someone tried to help the boy
                                                    across.

I've asked you what a Padre's for: well now I wonder, Bill
    If he's been sent by Jesus Christ to help us up the hill?
He's not a saint and yet it's grand, tho' some might think
                                                    it odd,
    That we should have a fellow here to make us think
                                                    of God.

K. W. Parkhurst

*Written when Padre with the Royal Welsh Fusiliers,1940.
Kenneth W. Parkhurst, Rev. MBE, HCF: Born Brighton
Trained for Baptist Ministry, Regents Park College. Army
Chaplain. After Dunkirk 1st Bn, Royal Welsh Fusiliers and
India and Burma with 14th Army.*
SEAC 24 June1945

To The X, The I, and The V

(Fourteenth Army — XIV)
(This monologue was composed for a show at Leeds given specially for relatives of SEAC men by the famous Yorkshire comedian)

You've heard of that green-eyed old idol, they say it was
near Katmandu,
The story to all is familiar, the sad fate of poor mad
Carew.
Had I the pen of a Kipling, my epic would have as it's theme
The deeds of the staunch Fourteenth Army, a saga of
jungle green.
Out there in tropical Burma, where existence is primitive,
grim,
Fight your husbands, your sons, and your brothers,
led by William the Conqueror Slim.
They live more or less just like Tarzans, for nature is cruel
and raw,
These old sweats of Imphal, Kohima, Tiddim, Tamu,
Myitkyina.
Hand-to-hand combat's the order, for the Japs are fanatical
foes
Ambitious to die for their Emperor, these treacherous
vile so-and-sos.
The B.O.R. with the Gurkhas, Punjabis, the Sikhs,
Dogras, Rajputs, and Jats,
Louis Mountbatten's vermin-destroyers, have slain
thousands of Tokyo's rats.
Chindits made famous by Wingate, Deep Penetrators
under Lentaigne,
The second, fifth, seventh Divisions, have won
themselves undying fame.
Christison, Reed, Festing, Gracey, Stopford, Messervy and
Scoones,
Roberts and Lomax and Cowan have smashed their way
through to Rangoon.

Admin Box, the Buthidaung Tunnels, Akyab, Nyakyedauk,
and Kabaw,
Ukhrul, Kanglatongbi and Palel, such victories will live
evermore.
Wiltshires, Royal Norfolks, and Suffolks, the Queens, York
and Lancs, Carabiniers,
Berkshires, West Kents, Worcesters, Lincolns, West
Yorks, Welsh and Scots Fusiliers,
Borders, the Devons, Northamptons, Royal Scots,
Seaforths, Cameron and Tanks.
Dragoons, the old Royal Sussex, the SWBs,
the Gloucesters and South and East Lancs,
I recall Chiang's men from China, Joe Stilwell's GIs by
Hukaung
Nagas and East and West Africans, stealthy, and skilful
and strong.
These are the names we must honour, a truly magnificent
Corps;
They all curse the snakes and mosquitoes, but they
curse 'soya links' even more.
The RAF bring them their rations, their airmail from friends
who are dear;
Parachutes from the skies drop them bully, the troops
wish they'd drop 'em some beer.
As I speak at this moment, the jungle is bathed in the light
of the moon,
But the boys long for new stars to gaze at, yes, more
stage stars would be a great boon!
We've made whoopee because of VE-Day, we have
linked up in Berlin and Rome,
But we pray for the X One and V Day
When the grand FOURTEENTH ARMY comes home!

Stainless Stephen

46.

THE SOLDIER'S LAMENT

So you were in the Navy, you won the war alone
  You didn't need the Army, but did it on your own.
We were already out there when the war began
  The powers that be said: 'Take a break and get a nice
                                           sun tan.'
You roughed it in your warships. Each day you took a bath
  Served up three good meals a day, would I change?
                              Don't make me laugh.
We all lived in luxury, in a hole dug in the sand,
  The bully beef and hard tack, a soldier's life was grand,
You didn't stay in one place long, you'd other calls to make
  Like Grant Road and El Benka, your own thirst to slake.
We'd eaten so much desert sand we thought it curry stews.
  So they sent us on to Burma, but only for the cruise.
You took us out there in your ships, your coverage did not slack
  But you'd a call to Civvy Street, and forgot to take us back.
Once again sheer luxury, but this time sleep neath trees
  To share our lot with nature, mosquitoes, snakes and fleas.
You had your daily tot of rum, more hardships without doubt,
  But should the occasion rise again, be sure to count me out.

Tom Kienzle

Sailor's Mickey

Yes, we were in the Navy, The Silent Service, mate.
　　We didn't win the war old son. You did it all . . . but wait
Who got you off at Dunkirk? You pongoes on the beach,
　　Three hundred thousand 'Brown Jobs', whipped out of
　　　　　　　　　　　　　　　　　　　　　　Jerry's reach.
　　Who took you back on June the sixth to let you try once
　　　　　　　　　　　　　　　　　　　　　　　　more?
You thanked us all by spewing up upon our messdeck floor.
　　And when you talk of desert sand, remember old
　　　　　　　　　　　　　　　　　　　　　　Tobruk?
Who was it brought your Bully Beef for your so called cooks
　　　　　　　　　　　　　　　　　　　　　to cook?
　　And then you mention hardships, you really make me
　　　　　　　　　　　　　　　　　　　　　　grin
For no one tasted hardships 'til they've tasted 'Herrings in'.
　　And then we come to 'Dekho' land, oh yes we got there
　　　　　　　　　　　　　　　　　　　　　　　too,
At Akyab, Myebon, Ramree, Letpan, and Old Kyauk Pyu,
　　And by the way old soldier, a phrase that's oft' been
　　　　　　　　　　　　　　　　　　　　　coined,
If you didn't like the Army you should not have bloody
　　　　　　　　　　　　　　　　　　　　joined.

L. O. Saleh
(Hello Sailor)

THE ROYAL AIR FORCE

You sound so very bitter against our Navy lads,
 You talk as if the army was the only force we had.
What about our boys in blue who flew night and day,
 They may have had their 'Brylcreem' but not a word
 they say.
You talk about our good life and daily tots of rum,
 No mention of our battles, no mention which we won.
Now my verse is over there's just one more thing to say
 They gave you your tomorrow, but they gave their
 today.

E. Booth.

ENSA

In the Burma Campaign where the food was quite plain
 There was one thing that couldn't be plainer;
There wasn't much beer, but the best kind of cheer
 Was the E – N – S – A Entertainer.
There's a very soft spot in the hearts of 'our lot'
 For the lads and lasses of ENSA,
Who left the UK an ocean away
 And went where the jungle was denser.
They'd fly out from Blighty with toothbrush and nighty,
 And land at Dumdum or Comilla;
Then with hardly a pause, to tremendous applause
 The show that they'd give was a thriller.

49.

They'd arrive in a Jeep, with a cheery 'Beep! Beep!'
And tramp through the mud and the muck –
Then give us a show, that would make the tears flow,
From the back of a three-tonner truck.
Though the past is quite hazy, who forgets
'Gert andDaisy'?
And wasn't Patricia Burke nice?
How we pressed to get nearer, to listen to Vera,
Who sang to us perched on a barrel,
And it really was painless to listen to Stainless,
And Forsyte and Seamon and Farrell.
There were so many more whom we used to adore
When we were out there in the forces.
We'd drive many a mile for a song and a smile
To follow the Stars in their courses.
So, to all of those 'Stars'
From all of us 'Stars'
Who served out in SEAC – All Ranks –
There's a message that's right,
And too short to be trite,
It's simply – 'We'd like to say, 'THANKS'

Ken Brown

The Reunion

Last night I went back thirty years,
When I was just a lad;
I lived again a thousand days,
Some good – some great – some bad.
And memories that time had dimmed
Came flooding through my brain,
A laughing face – an outstretched hand –
Yes, I was young again.

I saw once more the dark green hills
   Beneath the Burma sun,
I heard again the whistling shells
   And 'chatter' of the gun.
Filled to the ears with Mepacrine,
   Smeared with mosquito cream,
All dining on 'K' ration packs
   And garbed in jungle green.
We weren't the smartest troops on earth,
   For shine rubs off in mud,
And every foot of land we 'bought'
   The 'deeds' were 'signed' in blood.
I saw again Frank Simmonds fall,
   I watched Hugh Burden die,
Once more I felt the sting of tears
   But soldiers mustn't cry.
I knelt beside a hundred graves
   Much more than mounds of earth,
A 'link' with freedom each, for which
   A man gave all his worth.
And wrapped again in comradeship
   With men of every breed,
I felt the oneness that once was
   The Fourteenth Army's creed.
We didn't think of black or white
   Religions caused no fuss,
If you wore a battered bush hat
   Well, you were one of us.
I can't describe the feeling
   That made me ten feet tall
At the Burma Star Reunion
   Held in the Albert Hall.
There's just one point I'd like to make,
   One thing I'd like to say
Just how many 'Tomorrows' was
   The cost to have 'Today'?

By *a member of the Royal Sussex Regiment*

TO THE GURKHAS

It is so sad this tale I'm told
    About these men so brave and bold,
Small in stature but not in deed,
    For bravery has been their creed.
Through countless years they've helped
                      our cause
    And aided us through two world wars.
All this time they gave their best,
    Their courage always stood the test.
It makes us think they should never go,
    Our history books will prove this so,
Here's hoping that they won't disband,
    We're proud to see them in our land.

Anonymous

EAST FEVER

I must go back to the East again, to the burning tropical
　　　　　　　　　　　　　　　　　　　sky,
　And all I ask is a thousand chips, and the blazing sun
　　　　　　　　　　　　　　　　　　on high,
　And a good meal, and a cool drink and the hot ground
　　　　　　　　　　　　　　　　　baking,
　And a shimmering heat, which burns your feet, and a
　　　　　　　　　　　　　　　new dawn breaking.

I must go back to the East again, for the call of the Maiden
　　　　　　　　　　　　　　　　　　　wide
　Is a wild call and a clear call that cannot be denied;
And all I ask is a rainy day, with the black clouds flying,
　And the constant rain down the basha's drain, and the
　　　　　　　　　　　　　　　charwallah's crying.

I must go back to the East again, to the beetles, snakes and
　　　　　　　　　　　　　　　　　　　ants,
　To the hat-bush and the helmet-pith, and the natty khaki
　　　　　　　　　　　　　　　　　　pants,
And all I ask is a warm fire, and a bed as soft as clover,
　And some hot char from dear old Ma, when the
　　　　　　　　　　　　　　　nightmare's over.

M. B. W.

FIGHTER'S FESTIVAL

The Royal Sussex Regiment with whom I marched when
young
Were mighty men in battle – but could also loose the
bung.
Their deeds blaze back through history, from Pilkem to
Quebec,
But Sussex too, breeds trenchermen, built broadly at the
neck.

Their 'Spit and polish' soldiering shone brightly on parade,
And, facing odds in Picardy, they triumphed at their
trade.
But, whether back in billets or at home from war released,
The Royal Sussex warriors loved well a royal feast.
The burden of our blacked out years has dulled convivial
joys;
The scarlet and the silver seem like long discarded toys;
The guest-night and the band's brave airs, the ritual of the
Mess
Sort ill with an unlovely world that lives in battle-dress;
And therefore I rejoice to read of how the troops grew gay
Beside the Irrawady river, north of Mandalay.

They crossed the stream in sampans last December – some
time back
And there the leading company ran up the Union Jack;
They made their dispositions – outposts, picket, and patrol

– But, since the time was Christmas, they did honour to
the bowl.
The Royal Sussex Regiment had bacon, ducks, and geese,
And ale in which to pledge their King – five pints of it
apiece.

54.

Their Christmas Day was Church Parade, old carols sung
with zest,
Regatta for the sampan-crews, and football for the rest,
A pwe, with Burmese music – witching dancers, almond-
eyed –
The merry Royal Sussex – who can feast as well as fight.

Capt. A. W. Martineau
Who visited the Royal Sussex at Katha – Christmas 1944

Hell's Railway At The Going Down Of The Sun

To the south of Pakenbarue
    Where the nightly tiger prowls,
And the Simians greet the morning
    With their ululating howls,
Through the Kampong Katabule
    And the district of Kuban
There runs a single railway track,
    A monument to man.

In a short and fretful period
    That was eighteen months of hell,
Through the tangle of the tropics
    And the oozing swamps as well.
Through the cuttings that they hollowed
    And the embankments that they built,
They laid a modern railway line
    On jungle trees and silt.

And in spite of tropic noonday
    And a host of wasting ills,
Ever southwards went the railway
    To Mura and the hills,
Every sleeper claimed a body
    Every rail a dozen more,
T'was the hand of fate that marked them
    As it tallied up the score.

Thirty times a score of prisoners
    Fell asleep upon their backs,
Thirty times a score of prisoners
    Fell asleep beside the tracks,
Thirty times a score of times
    The sum of one immortal man,
Thirty times a score of cyphers
    In the councils of Japan.

On their ulcerated shoulders
    They transported rough-hewn wood,
With dying desperation
    Carried more than humans should,
On their suppurating feet
    With beri-beri swollen tight,
From the rising of the sun
    'Til the welcome fall of night.

From the rising of the sun
    Until the setting of the same,
Theirs was just a grin and bear it
    And pretend it was a game,
Theirs was to laugh and say
    They'd have a grill when it was done,
And the cooling breath of evening
    Took the place of scorching sun.

With the cooling breath of even
    Came a leaven of repose,
And a narrow hard unyielding bed
    On which to rest their woes,
Just a width of rotten bedboard
    For a shrunken, rotten frame,
Where the bliss of sweet oblivion
    Might eradicate the shame.

Let the bliss of sleep's oblivion
    Tarried long upon its way,
While bedbugs left their havens
    For a drying, dying prey,
And the ants and the mosquitoes
    And the scorpions and the lice,
Joined the rats and noisy chikchaks
    And the jungle lesser mice.

So another day was over
    And another day was done,
So another day of misery
    Was all too soon begun,
But the mighty Tenno Haika
    And the power of Japan,
Can't recall a day that's done with –
    And thank God there's none who can.

Show a leg my sleeping hearties!
    Oh, get up and rise and shine!
For the sky is blue and cloudless
    And they fear it would be fine,
There was breakfast for the hungry
    If their stomachs weren't too sour,
Made of boiling swampy water
    And of tapioca flour.

Back in England, paperhangers
    Would refuse the mess,
But Japan must give them something
    And it couldn't give them less,
So they thought of those who loved them
    And with far, unseeing eyes,
They consumed their mess of pottage
    And the maggots and the flies.

There was someone trusting somewhere
    That a husband would return,
There were sweethearts praying softly
    There were candle lights aburn,
There was God up in his heaven
    And he knew about it all,
And he heard their falt'ring whispers
    And he listened to their call.

And they drew new strength from somewhere
    And they battled for their life,
Though the odds were overweighted
    In this too unequal strife,
But they kept on carrying sleepers
    And they struggled with the rail,
And they persisted hopefully
    When it seemed to no avail.

It was "Kura" and "Canero" –
    If you straighten up you shirk,
And one excuse for living
    Is a finished job of work,
'Twas the mercy of the Emperor
    That saved them from the gun,
There was nothing now to save them
    From the task they had begun.

There was nothing then to save them
    From the toiling and the sweat,
But the saving grace of illness
    That was more exacting yet,
So they welcomed their malaria
    With its' vomit and its' ache,
So they welcomed their malaria
    For its semi-torpors sake.

There was dysentry, pellagra,
    And a host of sister ills,
Beri-beri and Bush Typhus,
    But no medicines or pills,
There was every cause for dying
    But few for hanging on,
When so many fell asleep and
    Followed comrades who had gone.

It was tie them in a hurry
    In an old discarded sack,
With a plank of rough cut timber
    To support them in the back.
It was lower them as gently
    As a withered muscle may,
And commend them to their Maker
    And remain a while to pray.

But for those they left behind them
    There were brutish things to bear,
At the hands of brutish beings
    Who were only well aware
Of the primitive upsurgings
    Of an animal delight,
That enjoyed the thrills of torture
    And the quiverings of fright.

They could drag their aching bodies
    To their grass and timber huts,
They could rub the salt of ampotanco
    In open weals and cuts.
They could steel their will to conquer,
    To forget, perhaps forgive,
But they found it mighty difficult
    To force themselves to live.

They had open huts of atap
　　Loosely tied to wooden poles,
And the roof and the partitions
　　Gaped and yawned in rotting holes.
Either side were filthy bedboards
　　But a yard above the ground
With a floor of earth and water
　　And with refuse all around.

And to rest their weary bodies
　　Overworked and underfed,
Sixty centis of this planking
　　Was their homestead and their bed.
Sixty centis night and morning,
　　Was the total – well or ill,
Sixty centis for each body,
　　It had to fit the bill.

Many talked of playing cricket
　　Many said they'd played the game,
But they let the devil rider
　　Take the honest and the lame.
There are many who'll be tongue-tied
　　When the trump of doom shall burst
On the ears of waiting sleepers,
　　On the blessed and the cursed.

On the twenty-ninth of April
　　There was nothing to be done.
On the birthday of the Emperor
　　They rose to greet the sun,
And his Clemency Imperial
　　Made a fatherly decree
That the slaves may send a postcard
　　To their wives across the sea.

When the day at last arrived
    And when the rest of them were free
They devised a Union Jack
    And displayed it on a tree,
And they thanked the God that made them
    That He let them live again,
And they prayed they might be better
    For the suffering and the pain.

There they left their friends behind them
    Thirty times a score or more,
Left them sleeping in the shadows
    On a distant tropic shore,
And I pray that God Almighty
    In the evening of their lives,
Will be gentle to their parents
    And their children and their wives.

Author unknown,
Pakenbarue, Sumatra, 1944

*It should be noted that Pakenbarue is on the Island of Sumatra and NOT in Burma. This poem is not written from the Burma Railway – which, for many reasons, and perhaps in particular the film **Bridge On The River Kwai**, is much better known as a construction undertaken by Allied POWs – although there is probably little difference other than the geographical location and perhaps in the number of POWs employed in the construction.*

Editor

Honi Soit Qui Mal Y Pense

Tell me, old friend, was it but yesterday,
    Or all those many, many years ago,
When we stood side by side on Burmese soil
    Searching the hazy distance for the foe,
Until his mortars belched into the sky
    Their bombs, which burst with little thunderclaps,
And you ducked, as the dust flew high,
    And said "God! How I hate the Japs!"
The intervening years have healed some wounds
    But some, again, will never be made whole;
How could a family ever be restored
    When one is but a name on Honour's Roll?
(Though these we hallow to Eternity
    With words engraved on stone so far away –
"When you go home, tell them of us and say,
    For your tomorrow we gave our today. . .")
Now that tomorrow is the present day;
    The peace for which our comrades paid the bill
Is ours – and but a memory are the names
    Of Arakan, The Admin Box, Jail Hill;
But can we be expected to forget
    And, more, forgive, that enemy with ease,
And welcome to our country as a guest
    The Emperor of all these Japanese?
Should our Chivalric Order be restored
    To him, who bears the name of "Heaven's Son",
If we could only put it to the vote
    Of those who died to face the Rising Sun –
And take a show of hands from those far graves,
    And take a count of those 'against' and 'for',
Remembering the Railway, Changi Jail,
    And those of Nippon's Prisoners of War!
It does not pay to nurture hate, they say;
    Neglected, soon it withers and grows cold;

Perhaps our hatred has abated now
    And we care less for enmities of old.
But – keep the faith with those we left behind;
    Remember them, remember why they stayed.
Even if we no longer hate the Jap,
    Should he receive this priceless Accolade.

***K. H. Brown*,**
1971, Brighton, Sussex.

My Garden

I had a garden of my own
    With fragrant flowers of every hue,
But the beauties I have known,
    Alas! have faded from my view.

The memories of sweet hours I've spent
    Amid the flowers at eventide
Were with me where so 'ere I went
    A thought of beauty by my side.

Such things of beauty linger long,
    Within my lonesome heart;
Living like a glorious song,
    Although we're far apart.

There'll come a day when I'll return,
    To that far distant shore,
And then no more my heart will yearn
    But rest in peace for evermore.

W. H. Slaney
Bangalore, 5 June 1944

In Our Own Time

Time bites into the waning year;
  Strong trees shudder in autumn winds,
Shedding their russet tears.
  Pointed sea-birds struggle on high;
Old men dream their dreams.
  Younger then, in summer's fulsome bloom
When turmoil swept us whither scheming,
  No time then for youthful dreaming,
Time but to grasp what life was there.
  Emerged soon our winter of violence,
Young saplings merged with jungle green,
  Étoliate, Yet strong in this emergence,
Perplexed by strange enchanted scene.
  The buds of Primavera have burgeoned oft
Since those half-forgotten days;
  Yes! ourselves forgotten too it seemed,
Remote from homeland in so many ways,
  Found stature greater than was dreamed.
Time now only to forgather
  In esoteric conclave, to reflect
On stirring times, avuncular inspiration
  Combined with youthful vigour,
Welded an army to command respect,
  Victory beams her precious light,
Yet demands propitiation;
  They lie there – far, far from friendly soil.
We, who saw their laughing youth,
  Remember – shall always remember.

  E. D. Portlock, BEM,
  Ex-Sgt. 9th Royal Sussex Regt.,
  36 Division

Waiting and Wondering

Waiting and Wondering
  When the day will come,
When we will see the glory
  Of the setting sun
Over England's hills and valleys
  As in the days of yore,
Living in contentment
  And in peace for evermore.

Waiting and Wondering
  When will come the time
That we will sit beneath the roses
  And hear the church bells chime,
Borne on an evening breeze
  So infinitely sweet
We will cherish all these moments
  When once again we meet.

Waiting and Wondering
  About a day that's new
Living in reality
  Of prayers and dreams come true,
Knowing all the joys
  We never knew before
Sharing our happiness
  And love for evermore.

W. H. Slaney,
71 Column, Chindits, (10 April 1944)

MEMORIES OF THE GOLDEN HOURS

The golden hours went all too soon,
  From the moment we first met,
Although they're gone and we're apart,
  Their memory lingers yet.

The sweetness of your face so dear,
  Which then was often close to mine,
Is with me yet, in these dark days
  A thought of beauty, so divine.

There'll come a day, when strife is o'er
  And the weary world turns to God for rest,
T'is then I will return to you
  The one I love the best.

Then once again the 'golden hours',
  Will be just as before,
But this time they will linger
  With us for evermore.

W. H. Slaney

November 1941

A CHINDIT

What was a 'Chindit'? the young ones say,
  When we are on parade, with badges on display;
Well, what else can an old soldier say? –
  Except long ago, we had our day;
We were 'yomping', before 'yomping' was ever invented,
  In Burma, a country, which never relented.

67.

Up that hill and down that plain,
    Bodies often racked with pain
Then up that cursed hill again
    Fearing for one's own sanity –
Nearly losing faith in God and humanity.

Sodden boots and rain soaked clothes,
    Not much chance of sweet repose
Of salty sweat dripping from one's nose
    And no-one smelling like a rose;
Still! there were men whose spirit rose.
On top of this there were the Japs –
    Crafty, persistent little chaps
Who didn't believe in giving slaps –
    But socked one, almost to collapse
And no matter what we gave
    They came back, as from the grave.

Every night a silent prayer –
    "Please God, let us be back where
Friends and loved ones, wait to share
    A life that's always free from care."

Some prayers were answered,
    And they came back –
To stand and think of Bert and Jack,
    Who shared Comradeship, Joy and Tears,
But stayed behind in those grim years.

> ***W. H. Slaney,***
> 2nd Leicesters, Ex-Chindit (71 Column)
> On the 40th Anniversary of the Chindit
> Campaign in Burma 1944

To Those We Left Behind

Black flies on the face of my comrade,
    As he lies face up to the sky,
Blue eyes staring fixedly
    Asking the question – in God's name why?

He lies so still with knees drawn up
    And hands across his breast,
As he did long years ago
    In his mother's womb, at rest.

He left his home and family
    A few short months ago,
Now here, he'll soon be sleeping
    In a grave they'll never know.

He did not know that one day
    We who survivied would stand heads
                    bowed and say –
"When you go home, tell them of us and say
    For your tomorrow, we gave our today."

Generation upon generation,
    Each strive against their kind,
They never seem to realise
    That no one is going to win.

Oh! would that God could grant us,
    A world that is free from greed
And give us strength and wisdom
    To help us in one's need.

W. H. Slaney, Ex-Chindit
2nd Leicesters, 71 Column.

Battles Lost Battles Won

They proudly march,
    We remember them,
Their medals pinned upon their chests.
    From miles and miles they have come,
Battles lost, battles won.

They march behind the standards bright,
    Aging bodies, failing sight.
The forgotten heroes, appear once more
    Remembering battles, on a far-off shore.

    Two minutes silence,
        tears are shed,
    All are remembered
        – The living and the dead.

    Thoughts are straying,
        Of sadness and glee,
    Those many emotions,
        Shared over the sea.

    Then away they march,
        And scatter like seeds,
    But proudly remembered,
        By you and me.

    We must never forget them,
        And to people we say,
    "For our tomorrow
        They gave their today."

Joanna Capon, age 14
Grand-daughter of the Rev G. G. C. Ridgway,
Plymouth Branch Padre.

THE BURMA STAR PARADE

Two hundred men go marching by,
    See how they raise their standards high;
These 'Burma Star Men', no longer young,
    To join their comrades here they come;
See how those medals shine in the sun,
    They were not given 'Just for Fun'.

Boys to the East, they sailed away,
    Through jungle, forest and decay,
A strange land to them and foreign ways,
    Songs of England in their heart always.
March to the band, hold your heads up high,
    Never mind the grey hairs, 'A gallant try',
Some were lost, now in our prayers,
    While the 'Burma Star' shines, 'Someone Cares'.

May Baker
Wife of a Wigston Burma Star member

THE FALL OF SINGAPORE
15 February 1942

On the day we were taken our spirits fell,
　And although 'twas not showing it was easy to tell,
After long days of fighting our chances were rare
　For something was missing – the boys of the air,
But our lads still kept on slamming the shells up the bore,
　Facing death from dive-bombers, and trench mortars galore,
Through all this destruction their spirits ranked high,
　Even when shells whistled mighty close by.

Still the lads carried on through long weary days,
　Helping the infantry in their short gruesome fight,
But the Japs were so numerous and ready to die,
　And kept on coming with help from the sky;
We bravely fought on, with our backs to the wall,
　And each soldier's heart-cry – the Isle must not fall,
Guns barked defiance with angry retort,
　And then came the whispers – ammunition is short.

The drivers set forth o'er the death-ridden lanes,
　Searching for 'ammo' amongst shattered remains,
But dumps had been seized by fifth column spies
　And they came back hurt, some with tears in their eyes.
Our shells were then numbered and handled with care,
　Each one went over and in turn did it's share,
Still we kept from each other that dreaded defeat,
　And prepared with fixed bayonets the enemy to meet.

We found with a shock that the water supply
　Had been seized from our grasp, and the taps had run dry,
The lads chatted gaily though we feared from their tone,
　That the hour had come and our last hope had gone.

That same afternoon, when expecting it least,
  We found on all fronts that the firing had ceased.
It wasn't the stillness that made us all stare,
  It was the white flag that caused our despair.

Then the order was given the enemy had won,
  Each stout heart was breaking like a true British son,
For we had fought hard for this small British isle,
  Ready to die to the last rank and file.
Now my thoughts wander back to the day that I kneeled
  By a small wooden cross near a battle scarred field,
To our comrades who died for that 'Isle' o'er the sea,
  That country! Our England! The Land of the Free.

Author Unknown

MEDITATION

Over Burma Dawn is breaking
  And the glory of the sun appears,
One more day of history making,
  One more day of sweat and tears.
To men of Burma long years ago,
  This was just another day,
With dreams of frost and crisp white snow,
  Green pasture lands and new mown hay.
For the lads who quietly lie,
  Burma proudly keeps their dreams.
Old soldiers really do not die
  They sleep for ever, calm, supreme.
Once more the dawn is breaking,
  Once more the glory re-appears,
But this is glory in the making
  Of Burma men down through the years.

G. E. Tilley

The following three pieces of prose or poetry were written by a young man who had been married in the Autumn of 1940, just prior to going out to India. They were written at the Royal Corps of Signals base in India before going into Burma and clearly give the feelings of a newly married man.

THOUGHTS ON RECEIVING A LETTER FROM HOME

'Yours of last year to hand . . .' This one you wrote
While the old year – with one day left to run –
With sirens shrill and screaming bombs distraught
Was heralding the New.
'Farewell to '40; hail to '41!' What terrors now,
What new peculiar forms
Of mental torture lie for us in store?
Are we to suffer now
The frank indignity of armed invasion, fraught
With all the horror tales of total war:
Am I to lack for months, nay years on end,
The constant comfort of my weekly mail?
Never to hear of days in school and nights in
                           gossip spent,
Of sewing parties, tea-cup chats, and scraps of news
                           of no account
To any soul but us . . . This day we saw a film,
                           – a funny film,
I commended it to you; the next we to the theatre went,
Where we enjoyed a first-rate show. . . Ah, lucky girl!
What joy to hear that you still live
As once we lived – and loved. It does me good
To hear you speak of these –
Such trivial, tame, inconsequential things
And know they still exist.
You make them seem so real – I see them still,

Tossed as I am on this far distant shore,
An exile in a barren land (who knows when to return?)

This is no pleasure cruise, no 'Land of Beauty' this –
The 'Mystic East' my foot!
This is a land of filth and poverty,
Of sweepers, beggars, lepers, dust,
Where white men fester, age and rust,
Where rich grow fat and poor men pine
And natives live in huts like swine,
Where in a dark and stinking hovel
Hindus and Moslems cringe and grovel,
And Fakirs beat themselves with rods
Just to appease their idle gods . . .

But soft! I lose myself. I know 'twould be
A Heavenly place if you were here with me.
Your letters are most welcome, chuck,
Transporting me to happier times, where I
– For a brief spell forgetting – think
Myself at home once more and by your side.
I could not wish for more. I cannot read too much.
Please write more often – and write more.

R. E. S. Clay
MHOR CI February, 1941

LINES DASHED OFF BEFORE BREAKFAST

Ah, happy days that once we knew, and happier nights,
    alas too few,
Such sweet, fantastic, far off days; it seemed we dreamed
    them in a maze
Of strange enchantment, while we faced
    The unknown future and time raced.
Lord! How time flew – and still we dreamed,
    And in the morning planned and schemed.

But did we dream of Kashmir snows or of that
                    Himalayan rose
Which blooms each year without our aid – say, did we heck!
We dreamed of home, that haven now so far away
Where we could think and have our say; –
Where given our allotted span we might have evidenced
                    a man,
– A man who now with martial spite is giving all to win
                    this fight,
– For what? we ask. 'Tis time we knew, is it for us,
                    for me and you?
Or is it just a sacred few who care but little if they spew
The blood of millions on the soil, provided that
                    their earthly toil
Does not besmirch their conscience? I say again if
                    I were home
Where working men are fairly free, to see once more
                    my native land
Where men are men and free to stand upon their feet
                    to face the foe,
Not marking time while others strive
                    to pull their chestnuts from the fire;
Where men are free to love just such as thee –
                    And who could love too much?
A fig for Lovelace and his honour – 'Tis thee alone,
Thou art Madonna, Circe, Helen,
                    Queen of Sheba and the rest.
I've seen the world, – such as it is, so please
                    I would come home and take my ease.

R. E. S. Clay
India, August 1941

VERSES AT BREAKFAST

My love is boundless like the floods
That lordly Indus pours around.
'Tis richer than the temple's gold they say at Amritsar
is found.
'Tis rarer than the KOH-I-NOR, or TAJ MAHAL where
pilgrims kneel,
And all the jewels of Mysore would not buy the half of
what I feel.
My love is mightier than the sight
Of Himalayan mountains' height;
'Tis lordlier than the Hindu Kush
Where snow-capped peaks their summits push
Into a clear and cloudless sky –
So clear it makes one gasp – 'But why?' – Why should
I have
To spend my time in this far off and tropic clime,
Where white men rule the tribes that once
In servitude and meek response
To Mogul rulers bowed the head,
And looked to them for rice and bread?
This is no place for such as I,
Who said, 'Why should the poor man die
To feed the rich with costly things
That from the stubborn earth he wins?'
I would I were at home with thee
Where English folk are proudly free.
Then would I show thee what is love
And rank thy beauty high above
Great Samarkand and Agra's pile;
And Kashmir's snows could melt the while,
And Ceylon's pearl of beauty rare
Drop in the sea – I would not care
If Khyber Pass were rent in twain,
So I were in thy arms again.

R. E. S. Clay, MHOR CI August 1941

77.

COMRADE

I met a man I've known for years,
    His face was drawn, his eyes aglaze.
He told me that his time was near.
    But in his soul there was no fear.

For in his prime he'd fought a fight
    To settle the conflict of human rights.
We owe so much to men like this;
    For we slept safe through darkest nights.
He got his wish that he would die
    Amongst those friends he cherished high.

Donald Reid

MISSING

Missing, so runs the message, but to those by right who
    loved him most,
Who knew him fully, as a mother knows, more truly
    was he lost –
Lost as a child – he was so young in years – who strays
    within a crowd
And wanders helpless (hurt maybe), in tears, calling
    her name aloud.

As once a child from his fond parent's care did wander forth
    alone
Yet was discovered by the anxious pair after three
    days were gone,
Such is the ancient story, and the thing for comfort comes
    to mind
That so we may too seek him sorrowing, hoping, like
    them to find.

J. H. F. McEwens   1944

78.

Auxiliary Hospital: 1944

Lord, what are we, that these should pay
   Such price of pain, for us to stay
Safe and at ease, beyond the reach
   Of armed assault along the beach?
To save us from the fate of slaves,
   These, by a fraction, missed their graves,
To sweat with pain and lie awake
   For our most undeserving sake.
Like thee, they pay too great a price;
   We are not worth such sacrifice;
With shame, we watch them joke and grin,
   Nailed on the cross of others' sin.
Oh Christ, who also bled and died,
   Look down on these Thy crucified;
On women, dumb beneath their loss,
   And us, blind fools, who built their cross.

Ruth Hedger 1944

I Shall Remember

Here, while the red hibiscus hangs its head
   Through all these sunshot 'winter' days,
Rich with colour light has shed
   On field and flower, on grass and sandy ways;
Here, as December days so warmly pass,
   I shall remember . . . cold days of Christmas.

Here, when the sun's last flush is swiftly gone,
   I shall see such myriad stars above
As on the lonely shepherds must have shone
   When first began the story of Christ's love;
And, creeping from shadowed trees, will seep scents
   More subtle than of myrrh or frankincense.

Then shall I recall a snowclad night
  In England, and the heap'd fire's light
Flickering on faces happy with sound
  Of old music, bright with 'glory shone around'.

A. A. Steele
RAF, India, Christmas 1944

MEMORIES
SEAC 25 December 1944

Christmas at home, what memories that brings:
  When we were children and our joys
Were centred round our gifts – the toys
  We used to get, the simple things
That gave us pleasure then.

Christmas! the focal point of happiness;
  The concentration of goodwill;
The proof that in our hearts is still
  A knowledge of Christ's holiness;
The synonym of peace.

Peace, in the midst of war – incongruous thought
  And yet why should I think it strange?
For in our hearts we do not change.
  And though in many lands we've fought,
Our hearts were never there.

Though we are here, our hearts are with you still.
  Christmas to us means peace to come,
The joy of returning home,
  The hope of future world goodwill,
The love we bear for you.

J. W. Nevill 25th December 1944

On The Spot

Visiting this land of sunshine
   Turned my thoughts to healthy tan.
(Handsome men are slightly sunburnt!) –
   Then my fiery test began.

Days of warmth grew ever warmer,
   Shade recordings rose apace;
Tidal pools of perspiration
   Made my feet an island 'base'.

Lo, a cloud (Man's-hand dimensions)
   Now appeared upon my sight;
Just an itch; I shrugged my shoulders –
   Till I tried to sleep that night!

Fifty million red-hot needles,
   Dipped in mustard, formic tipped,
Scorched and seared my burning body,
   Till it seemed the skin was stripped.

While my lucky friends were sleeping
   (Heartless blighters) in their cots,
Tenderly I made inspection –
   Found myself a mass of spots.

Spots on 'tum' and spots on elbow,
   Spots on back and spots on knee
Spots on wishbone, spots on toto,
   Spots of every pedigree.

Certain spots had high ambitions,
   Which, alas, I failed to foil;
First they simmered, then they bubbled,
   They they all began to 'boil'.

Kindly doctors clustered round me,
    Looked me over, head to feet,
Swiftly diagnosed my trouble –
    'Just a spot of prickly heat',

Then the men who study figures
    (Having records new in mind)
Studied mine, and took a census
    Counting spots of every kind.

Giving up at thirty thousand
    Claiming it too hard to see,
On my variegated torso,
    Which was spot and which was me!

Now I know the power of sunshine,
    Count me now a hardened 'sweat',
Thick with calomine and talcum,
    But the spots are with me yet.

Prickly heat has double action,
    Test it if these spots you catch;
Whilst it saps your vim and vigour,
    Yet it keeps you up to 'scratch'.

H. C. Bear

TEMPORARY SOLDIER

Today I am a soldier: give me not
    The pleasures and the sympathies I knew
But let me rest contented with my lot
    The char and wad, the never-ending queue.
I do not beg the touch of human love
    Cast not before my gaze the lustrous pearl,
Nor call upon my thoughts to rise above
    The ancient barrack yarn, the pin-up girl.
Today I am a number in the ranks
    Give me my mail and I am satisfied,
'Free tea for Troops' is poured upon my pride.
    But on the morrow, when the bugle blows,
I'll cast my boots and battledress away
    Resume my civvy shoes, my civvy clothes,
And men will listen to the things I say.

Frolik 1944

INTERCESSION

Whose hand the force that leads through fields of space
    And lays me prostrate where no comrade lies?
How soft the dust of days to knees and face!
    The silence has the weight of stifled sighs.
A flame – a wing – cuts through the nameless waste
    The trembling void recedes, no longer void,
Behold, the waves of life; and men employed
    On churning up the waves in mortal haste.
Lord God of Hosts, in this their blindest hour
    Keep guard of all whom doubt or dread devour;

Of men with bodies torn, or spirit splayed
   And mourners, taut of mouth, in yew-trees shade;
Of slaves who desecrate the hero's grave,
   And cringing crooks, and dupes who sin to save;
Of misers hiding crusts in slug-stained pots
   And hungry gleaners crooked in barren plots,
And wastrels on the mind, grown deaf and blind,
   Who dare not go ahead or lag behind,
Of all who deem themselves from light debarred,
   Lord God of Hosts, throughout their night, keep guard.

                           Julia Da Beausobre   1944

JUNGLE SCENE

Down in the jungle something stirred,
   It might be a Jap or it might be a bird.
I cock up my rifle and silently creep
   Into the undergrowth thick and deep.

I come to a clearing and suddenly see
   Tiny bells swinging from every tree,
Bluebells and buttercups on the ground
   With fairy folk dancing all round.

I pinch my arm and I rub my eyes,
   O hark to the joyful fairy cries,
Mark how the foxgloves gently sway
   To join the fairies in their play.

I put up my rifle and quietly withdraw
   And a gruff voice asks me what I saw
'Fairies, dear Sergeant' I make reply,
   And that's how I got seven days RI.

                                Frolik   1944

Bengal Blues

When I am old and time has drawn a veil
　Across these dreary miserable years,
And all the toil and sweat, the blood and tears
　Are but the trappings of a well-worn tale.

When in some sombre Monday-morning mood
　Tempted, I view old things in new disguise,
Raising time-tinted glasses to dim eyes
　That all but pleasant memories exclude.

Then let me see it all as clear as now;
　The muddy desolation of the scene,
Rain sodden skies above the weary green,
　And feel the weight of exile on the brow.

So as I watch the gentle English rain
　I shall find sweet contentment once again.

H. L. Robinson　1944

Unforgotten Men

The clouds on the hills are slowly dropping
   As day draws closer into evening,
Among the mists of Manipur.

The waterfall and the wild birds' call
   Are all that are left to mark the fall
Of those who fought and died among
   The wild grey mists of Manipur.

Many a brave heart is sleeping –
   No longer touched by lure of gold or laughter –
Among the hills of Manipur

They sleep eternal, calm and deep,
   Beneath the rocky hillside steep,
A ghostly shroud their only keep –
   The cold grey mists of Manipur.

                J. Risholi   1944

Evening in Manipur

Soft hills aglow with gold
   Ever-changing light –
Gay yellow dying slowly
   To a russet glow.
Flushed and painted sky –
   Bright golden clouds
Reflecting warmly
   On the world below.
Mauve hyacinths
   Among the wayside grass,
Wide lonely plains
   Of chequered golden green:

This beauty all too swiftly dies
    As twilight fades
And shadows cover hills
    Where light has been – But stay
Rising behind yon eminence the silver moon
    Lights Manipur anew with lovely radiance.

E. D. P. 1944

JUNGLE NIGHT

The man with the green cigarette strolls down the path
  Waving it in the air in conversation.
The man with the tiny anvil strikes it softly like a bell –
  Tink-tink: tink-tink.
The man with the dark blue cloak goes quietly by.
  There goes the man with the green cigarette again.

They are not really there. You know quite well
  They are not there.
Then one of them whistles softly.
  You finger the trigger of your Bren,
Half-fearing half-desiring the sudden hell
  Pressure will loose.
You listen – nothing – then
The man with the green cigarette strolls by again
  Waving it in the air.
Down comes the dew, Drip-drip: drip-drip.
  The man with the tiny silver anvil
Strikes twice; strikes twice.
  Softly passes the man with the cloak of blue:
Fireflies: Bell-birds: Shadows: Japanese.

"K" 1944

LIFE IN BURMA

(With apologies to Rudyard Kipling)

If you can stick the climate out in Burma,
  The blazing sun and dust that fills your eyes,
Your mouth and nose and throat when you are marching,
  The biting of mosquitoes, ants and flies;
If you can dream of home and all your loved ones,
  Of tasty food, and Mother's apple pie:
If you can still eat bully beef and biscuits,
  If you can starve and yet refuse to die;
If you can make your home in tiny dug-outs
  And little fox-holes cut into the ground,
If you can suffer boredom, uncomplaining
  And do two hours 'Stag' without a sound;
If you can keep your head with Japs all round you
  And everyone is getting in a 'flap':
If you can keep alert, awake and ready
  And hold your fire, then blow them off the map;
If you can wait for mail that's not arriving,
  Continuing to write your letters home,
With confidence that sometime in the future
  You'll be returning – never more to roam:
If you can fill each unforgiving minute
  With ninety seconds worth of distance run;
Yours is the stuff that makes a SEAC soldier,
  And what is more you'll beat the Rising Sun.

R. Payne   1944

BARBED WIRE

*(This poem was written by a rating on HMS Malaya to his
brother, who was a prisoner of war in Germany.)*

Daylight again, and still the night goes on,
  A dream that knows no waking.
Still we stare
  Beyond the wire to the old world we knew
Long since, when Life itself was fair.
  And each new daybreak with the spreading light
Brought us the gift of one more day to spend –
  To spend the way we would with song and friend
And well loved hills to wander – God how bright
  And clear the water ran in the dales of Wye.
Where primrose hides and dark trout haunts the stream
  And crazy walls go clambering to the sky,
Cloud-envious as we. I dare not dream
  Too much of that far world;
God give me strength
  To keep the one small flame of hope alight,
Defying this our dark, until at last
  The one Tomorrow comes and all is bright.

Michael Kelly 1944

THE 42ND BURMA REMEMBERANCE PARADE
24 April 1988

I would like to have applauded,
   But I knew I could not,
Standing to attention, rigid, straight backed,
   Steeled by the long remembered practices
And disciplines of a military past.

The soft spring sun glows on the gold
   Of the standards, erect and proudly borne
By their green beretted veteran bearers.

We had come from the four corners
   Of the Kingdom to honour our comrades,
To fulfil this moment of homage to those
   Who lie in an alien soil, in a distant land,
The men of Burma.

They endured the unendurable,
   Gave the manner of living
For a regiment in the service of their country,
   Gave their sweat, their blood,
And when there was nothing left to give
   They gave the ultimate, they gave their lives.

Theirs was the final sacrifice and gift
   To those who came after to pursue their lives,
In uninhibited freedom, unfettered by
   The domination of an unrelenting conqueror.

90.

We had assembled in the presence of history
 On Horse Guards Parade and marched off towards
The Cenotaph by supportive Royal Marine NCOs
 Calling the step like an echo from the past.
Rank upon rank, six columns long,
 Twin Royal Marine bands, their stirring cadences
Giving new vigour to aged legs.

Now we stand here in silence at the Cenotaph,
 The bugles call, the laying of wreaths,
The lowering of the standards,
 Emotions subdued and controlled before
The massed gaze of onlookers.

We shall remember you, our comrades-in-arms,
 And the brotherhood we shared, borne of adversity
And bonded in victory.
 And those of us who can, will page
And immortalize your names,
 Blazoned like those of royal kings,
For all to read and wonder.

E. F. Willmoth

THE UNWRITTEN LAW OF ALLEGIANCE

Trumpets are sounding for the time is at hand
 When men will be gathering from many lands;
Stars will be shining on each man's breast
 For tonight they pay homage to comrades at rest.

Amid the throng a man stands tall
Among many heroes at the 'Albert Hall'
And with eyes of compassion a word here and there
He will remember with pride – when he was called
to care.

His men had fought in the war long gone
On the seas, in the air, and a road so long,
For when hearts were heavy in their deepest plight
He gave them the courage to 'Fight the Good Fight'.

From the jungles of Burma their Star was born
To grow in its brilliance when nights were forlorn.
Their voices now one – Their 'Supremo' is near
And the rafters will shake with an Almighty Cheer.

With devotion unique they recall how it happened
At the Night of the Year with —
Lord Louis Mountbatten
Of Burma.

Edna May Farraro
South Croydon Branch
and Pinwe Club Member, 1979

PORTLOCK'S FOURTEENTH ARMY

Despairs gloomy countenance
Reflects on Burma's soil,
Deceptive perspective which seems to enhance
A land of rugged beauty, an ideal foil,
Yet hidden beneath such subtle veneer,
Encyclopaedic evils rear.

I know who can appreciate beauty,
    The misery of the rains, ravaging
This land, so green and wide,
    No man amongst us who can hide,
Tho' well he knows his task,
    Deep feelings of despondency
When the earth is fighting too.

Tormentors in myriads
    Attack from foetid soil,
With no respite for periods
    The men who sweat and toil;
Winged pests and crawling
    At darkness come, unseen
In daylight – when dusk is falling
    Blight of things unclean.

Microbic pestilence
    Wreaking deadly toll
Defying the diligence
    Of scientific role,
Sapping human energy,
    Strong and weak alike,
Unseen, intangible,
    Yet cunning, surely strike.

Dame Nature takes her deadly toll
    Yet tho' odds stacked high against us,
Grimly an army finds its soul
    The growing, sarcous epitomy
Of tenacity, belief and hope
    In ultimate victory
O'er Man's depravity and earth alike,
    For simple consummation of a simple joyous life.

Ed Portlock, BEM
Ex-Sgt 9th Royal Sussex Regiment

Our Padre

Our Padre – Captain, The Reverend Sparrow –
   Traversed the jungle tracks however narrow,
With the leading troops he would go,
   Not for him to wait or follow,
Always giving comfort to those in pain,
   And helping our 'Medics' life to maintain;
Carrying his 'Vestments' everywhere,
   For in Holy Communion he chose to share
His blessings with those who wished
   To partake of the 'Blessed —
Sacrament', and for those who only came to pray
   He would help them too in every way;
He was more than a blessing in disguise,
   For he was cheerful, willing and wise.

(Sandy) H. E. Williams (Ex-Sgt)
9th Bn The Royal Sussex Regt.

Kohima '44

I do not grieve for the men who fell at Kohima,
   They would disdain my tears,
I saw the young men, trailing their arms,
   Move off to the position on the spur,
And a great grief seized me
   For I knew that some would die.
But to live like a man, even for a short while,
   Is great and enviable;
Better than a life of bars
   And dogs and strikes and doles.
The undistinguished private in the ranks,
   As he advances up the hill,
             Lives like a man.

J. Gent — 3 September 1945

Skipper's Farewell

Toll for SEAC – Tomorrow's news today,
  For now it is off – 'tis doomed to fade away,
No more we'll greet the coming day
  Cheered by that bright Good Morning,
Heading words of wisdom hatched by newsmen of
                            letters
  Who seek to free us from the fetters
Of mental inexactitude, and turn our thoughts to all
                          things good.

Toll for the brave, the Fourteenth Gang of Rips
  Who put it well across the Nips;
Mowed them down in fields of paddy,
  Soused them in the Irrawaddy.
From Mandalay to Singapore,
  From Howrah Bridge to Old Johore.
Outgunned, outfought, the Rising Sun is flat aback,
  And going on the other tack.

Cheers for Mountbatten, who by strategy
                        and stealth,
  Drove all the Nips from Burma,
Here's bumper to his health.

In the middle of the campaign he hit upon a ruse
  He called upon Frank Owen, to give the boys
                        the news.
Said he to Frank, Come off that tank
  And lay your pistol down.
You're off to do the job for me, in Far Calcutta Town.
  The pen is mightier than the sword,
And words when well directed
  Will play their part, to cheer the heart,
And gladden the distracted.

I have no wit that makes me fit
    To write a full edition,
Or try to tell how heroes feel
    Amid the storm of shot and shell
When pounding all the Nips to Hell;
    There is however this to say,
That years from now when things are gay,
    And men foregather at the local
To spend their unemployment pay,
    You're sure to hear among their crack
Someone quoting from SEAC.

A. W. Kane, Master Mariner

THE EPISODE OF THE BOREHOLE SQUARE

It was in Prison Camp, under Japanese control,
We were ordered to sign the death warrant parole.
A non-escape form , with the penalty, Death –
But on all p.o.ws. they wasted their breath.

For as true British soldiers, the order refused
And by all their threats we were highly amused.
Our duty quite plain, was to try to escape,
So Japanese orders became second-rate.

But alas, as White people, we had not realised
These captors of ours were but half civilised,
For the treatment came which made us all stare
When we found ourselves quartered on Selerang Square.

In an area where under eight hundred had been,
Sixteen thousand were packed to make up this scene,
And there in this hell with space but to stand
We digested discomforts for the sake of our land.

No water to wash and little to drink,
Our problem of sanitation made us all think,
For there in the midst of this human throng,
Our latrines had been dug with plenty of song.

'Twas in these latrines that we took special pride
For here General and Private sat side by side,
And laughed and made joke of their fate that September,
An experience, I'm sure, all ranks will remember.

Scores of Jap sentries, alert to all sounds,
Had orders to shoot all men 'out of bounds'.
But we were all cheerful and happy to know
Our true British spirit was once more on show.

Epidemic disease gave us quite a fright,
For no movement of troops, whatever their plight.
No admission to hospital, no treatment at all,
No movement of dead, who had heard their last call.

Then we heard with a shock which disgusted us all,
That the Sikhs, who'd been British just prior the fall,
Were ordered to shoot four lads who'd escaped
Whilst commanders were ordered to watch how they shaped.

Quite cheerful and cool were those lads as they spoke
And bade their goodbyes to all Army folk.
Their blindfolds rejected, was brave you can tell,
As they watched rifles aimed, they saluted 'Farewell'.

So back to the Square which to us had been
The Borehole of Calcutta, all over again.
Where sing song and mirth simply filled the air,
As our boys in high spirits put the Japs in despair.

Author unknown (From F E Dow Mag.)

THE GREEN BERET

Men who heard the battle cry
Fearless men, who'd fight and die,
Men who meant just what they'd say,
Warriors of the Green Beret.

Wearing Fourteenth Army Crest
And divisional tabs, they were the best,
They wear the Burma Star today
Those valiant men of the Green Beret.

Trained to fight in a savage land,
Facing combat, hand to hand,
Men who fought in yesterdays,
And proud to wear their Green Berets.

And as they fought, to God they prayed
"Dear God above, give us this day,
Give us the strength to win this fight
And put our enemy to flight".

And those who fought, side by side,
'Neath burning sun and Eastern skies,
Can proudly stand and say today
"We were the men of the Green Beret".

And in England, they are free,
They recall battles across the sea,
Britannia, can proudly say
"God bless the men of the Green Beret".

A. J. Sambrook, TD,
PRO and Parade Marshal, Burma Star Association,
Birmingham Branch, Corporation Street,Birmingham 4

The Chindits Dream of Home

Take me where wild roses grow,
Into the lanes of dear old England;
Take me where the cool streams flow,
And on the briar sweet roses grow.

Roses white, and roses pink:
I see them in my dreams of England;
In the chain they form a link,
Sweet roses white, and roses pink.

But, I am a soldier here,
Fighting in the jungles of Burma;
We can never show our fear,
The enemy is ever near.

Snakes and poisonous spiders roam,
Monsoon weather is soaking us through,
Leeches make our bodies their home,
And fleas are nesting on my dome.

Some of us are very ill
With malaria and dysentry –
Don't forget to take your pill:
You're not much use if you can't kill!

Oh yes, I do sweet flowers see,
Exotic blooms grow in the jungle,
But I am no longer free
To let a flower influence me.

Will I ever cross the foam
To see again the rose of England,
Settled, never more to roam,
With all my folks and friends back home?

P. Puscty (Wife of Chindit)

99.

THE TAKING OF THE HILL

Sleep well my comrades, sleep,
The battle's won. I weep
To see your life's pulse cease
In mute eternal peace.

Brave hearts! I see you still,
Storming the flame swept hill,
Unsheathed your bayonets bare,
Dull in the morning air.

Death from sky, death from ground,
Shot and shell all around,
Through drifting smoke yet dim,
They tottered on death's rim.

No time to turn about,
No time to dwell in doubt,
Dear God in you we trust,
Dust triumph over dust.

They stumble, sway and reel,
Earth flies beneath the heel,
Guns hammer in the ear,
The wavering lines draw near.

They curse through gritted teeth,
Charge at the foe beneath
The shattered stumps of trees,
And crumple to their knees.

I stand alone barehead,
Among these honoured dead,
But will the World forget,
The sacrifice and debt?

E. F. Willmoth, Burma 1943

O BURMA STAR

(Can be sung to the tune of Genevieve)

O, Burma Star, O, Burma Star,
   How bright and clear and kind you are,
Shining on us near and far.

O, Burma Star, O, Burma Star,
   The light that shone on Imphal's plain
Must never wax and never wane,
   Kohima's message still must stay;
'For your Tomorrow, our Today'.

O, Burma Star, O, Burma Star,
   How bright and clear and kind you are,
Shining on us near and far.

O, Burma Star, O, Burma Star,
   Though time may cool the heat of hate,
Though years the passions may placate,
   Yet lives the dream of those who say,
'For your Tomorrow, our Today'.

O, Burma Star, O, Burma Star,
   How bright and clear and kind you are,
Shining on us near and far,
   O, Burma Star, O, Burma Star.

*The words were written by a blind friend member of St.
Helen's Branch.*

101.

ECHOES OF WASHINGTON DC

Many present at St Dominics' Church, Washington, on 18 October 1981 on the occasion of the dedication of the Standard of the First American branch were so impressed by the Address given by the Rev. J. F. Titus Oates, that it was felt the text should be recorded.

He said:

"It is a great honour to take this service today. I am honoured to have been asked, and as I take my part my heart is full of pride, pride in the great country in which I was born and pride in the great country of my adoption. Thank you for the honour you do to me in allowing me to take part in this great act this day.

Listening to the news, watching the news, or reading the newspaper can be very depressing business these days. All one seems to hear are acts of violence, hatred and we all grow weary of man's inhumanity to man.

We hear of violence and murder committed by self-seeking men thinly disguised under the veil of patriotism. We see the horrors of racism, not only in South Africa, but in the streets of the United States as well as in Great Britain. We see religious intolerance and bigotry as the great country of Ireland tears itself apart with Protestant and Catholics murdering and maiming each other. We see discrimination between peoples of different classes, different beliefs, different sexes, and different political positions. Yes, we see violence is everywhere. However, this day as we dedicate this Standard of the First American branch of the Burma Star Association, I see there is hope. For fighting in Burma, and standing shoulder-to-shoulder, and making up membership of this Association we have men and women of every nationality – not here for the glory of any one country, but united together in the spirit of the Association. We have blacks and we have whites, we have Irish Catholics and Irish Protestants, we have Conservatives, the Liberals and the Socialists, Republicans and Democrats, we have rich and poor, we have Christian, Jews and Atheists – men and women of every possible sort come together to form the BURMA STAR ASSOCIATION.

Perhaps this day should be a day of renewal of hope for all of us – for we should leave here knowing that peace and brotherhood, and service, are not just pipe-dreams, but are attainable. Surely what brought about the Spirit of the Burma Star Association is the bonding that came about when we all faced something that seemed almost too much for us. This sense of inadequacy did away with all false prides, and we were all humbled and brought to a knowledge that we could win through only with the help of God and the help of our fellow men and women, and it mattered not a hoot whether that person was British or American, black or white, Catholic, Protestant, Jew or Atheist. Perhaps that is where the spirit we share comes from, and I hope we will all go home to take the message that won us through in those dark days in Burma can win us through the dark times that we face today. We must indeed love God with all our hearts, and souls, and minds, and strengths, and this must lead us on to love our fellow men. Too often all we do is to talk about our love for our fellow men, and those of us who are Christians are as bad as those who are not.

We are so busy loving God, that we forget to love our neighbours – we are so heavenly minded that we are no earthly use. Our love for others must be real, not just lip-service, not a shallow and false bon-homie, without any reservations. This was the spirit of true religion, and the spirit of this Association will bring peace where there is hatred and distrust. Only when together we face something or someone greater than ourselves can we hope for nations to be truly united, and love and service to become a reality.

How do we do that? 'It begins with me.' I hope each of you will say it, and mean it.

"Now go your ways, and make it happen."

Taken from the Summer 1977 Dekho

About 450 Burma Star Association Members with some wives travelled to the 'States' to witness this dedication and enjoyed a most sincere welcome and stay. A true exhibition of togetherness and comradeship.

The Reverend Titus Oates was born in Great Britain and had served in the Royal Navy.

103.

THE ANNUAL REMEMBRANCE PARADE
(A Tribute to our late Supremo)

From the four corners of the Earth they came
To rally with comrades native to these Isles;
The spacious 'Horse Guards' for ageing 'Stars' a fitting frame;
Those eyes are bright, and steady stand the files.

A Band of Brothers, forged on sea, on land and in the skies
Against a common, deadly foe; remote from Home
They stand, six thousand strong, with alert eyes,
Proud and content to know they aren't alone.

St James' clock from centre turret strikes,
The rousing blare of music leading columns through
Admiralty Arch, around to Whitehall, keeping step alike,
Each man aware a martial bearing's due.

And so they form around a Nation's Shrine,
The 'Last Post' sounds, the 'Epitaph' to read;
We think of Comrades, even so long dead.

But they are with us, young, whilst we grow old;
'Reveille' stirs us from our thoughts, the tribute wreath is laid
A 'Benediction' given – the music strikes up bold,
We march before the Abbey and back to the Parade.
Once more the columns pass beneath a Leader's gaze,
A sharp "Eyes Left!" salutes him as of yore;
No doubts, we see the pride that fills his face
At Veterans loyal, alike in Peace and War,
Worthy to know, a credit to this Race.

J. F. O., 1981

NB. The above poem was incorporated on parchment scrolls in
Gothic lettering, on oak wooden stocks embossed with gold
stars by an American Burma Star CBI Veteran friend.

104.

THE MAN WITH THE RIFLE

Men may argue forever on what wins their wars,
    And welter in cons and pros,
And seek for their answers at history's doors,
    But the man with the Rifle knows.

He must stand on the ground on his own two feet,
    And he's never in doubt when it's won,
If it's won he's there; if he's not, it's defeat,
    That's his test when the fighting is done.

When he carries the fight, it's not with a roar
    Of armoured wings spitting death,
It's creep and crawl on the earthen floor,
    Butt down and holding his breath.

Saving his strength for the last low rush,
    Grenade throw and bayonet thrust,
And the whispered prayer before he goes in,
    Of a man who does what he must.

When he's attacked, he can't zoom away,
    When the shells fill the world with their sound,
He stays where he is, loosens his spade
    And digs his defence in the ground.

The ground isn't ours till he's there in the flesh,
    Not a gadget, nor a bomb, but a man,
He's the answer to theories which start afresh,
    With each peace since wars began.

So let the wild circle of argument rage,
    On what wins as war comes and goes,
Many new theories may hold the stage,
    But the man with the Rifle knows . . .

Author unknown

105.

The Forgotten Army

Where are they now the men so true?
   Where are they now the men so few?
Where are they now? Did someone say who!
   They gave their youth for me and you.

Maybe tomorrow or the day after.
   Amid a few tears or even laughter.
People will shout or even murmur.
   Where are the men, the men of Burma?

G. Roebuck

Harry's Comrades

They marched into darkness, into the unknown,
   They marched all together, yet each was alone.
The land which they travelled, they knew to be BURMA,
   Yet the only reality was terra firma.

They were all young and confident, but a little naive...
   If they had been told, they would not have believed,
The horror, the hardships, the loss, the pain
   That they were to suffer in this BURMA Campaign.

They fought through the jungle, the plains and the hills,
   Their success was measured by the number of 'kills'
Through Monsoons, the dust and unbearable heat,
   Their life of purgatory was almost complete.

The snakes and the leeches they endured with ease,
   Their biggest problem was the vile Japanese.
They learned to cope with the mad Samurai
   The little yellow b • • • • • • who wanted to die.

106.

They finally stopped the Japs' headlong drive
    And once and for all cut them right down to size.
It was here at KOHIMA, now etched in their hearts,
    Where the beginning of the end actually did start.

The battle was furious, the cost was so high,
    The Battalion fought well but a lot of them died.
With courage and bayonet and cast-iron will.
    They chased the Japanese off Garrison Hill.

Bunker by bunker, by night and by day,
    They pushed on from KOHIMA to old MANDALAY.
They conquered each strong point with bayonet and gun,
    And hastened the end of the vile 'Rising Sun'.

The 'Forgotten Army' of Slim's fighting men,
    Who had hammered the Japs again and again.
They left a Memorial made of white stone,
    On it was a message for all to take Home.

The message is simple, made without fuss,
    WHEN YOU GO HOME TELL THEM OF US AND SAY
The ultimate line is the one to obey.
    "FOR YOUR TOMORROW, WE GAVE OUR TODAY".

And still these men of the 'BURMA STAR',
    March together, from near and far.
They no longer march into the unknown,
    They walk in the Golden Light,
                Of the glory They have Known.

                  Bill Ridley
                  ex-DLI

At the 56.5 Milestone
– Dimapur to Imphal Road

You may talk about the sailor who sailed the seven seas,
   Or the pilot of the RAF who flashes through the breeze,
Or the lonely AA gunner on a barren British shore,
   Or a warden of the ARP – a product of this war.

You may talk about the miner who brings up the coal each day,
   Or the pretty little ATS whose job is far from play,
Or the grimy factory worker on a night shift at a bench,
   Or a fireman in an air raid 'midst the flames and smoke and
                                stench.

I must admit that I admire the way they carry on
   These fighters of old England and the uniforms they don,
But what about the Royal Scots now in a foreign land,
   Away from home and things they love and life they
                            understand.

Their struggle in the jungle against old Johnny Jap
   To keep that little bit of red on the British Empire map,
The marching through the mud and rain, the slogging up the
                              hills
   With little room for rations but lots for yellow pills.

The tackling of the bunkers well dug by cunning foes
   This task is pretty hefty as every Royal knows
The storming of the ridges and subsequent high hopes
   Soon blasted to eternity by fire from reverse slopes.

The shots from cunning snipers well hidden in the trees,
   Unseen by resting soldiers when they have a moment's ease,
The odd reports from 75s when everything seems calm,
   It very often is the case that these do lots of harm.

108.

The capturing of the villages or the mopping up of tracks,
   The sweat that's caused by carrying those far too heavy
                                                          packs,
The horror of road travel in a crowded army truck,
   The pitching of the two-men tents in any kind of muck.

The pains that come from colic when the dinner meal is passed,
   Those times when every minute seems bound to be your last,
The indent from the BID that's very seldom sent
   And the promises in SEAC that are never even meant:

The whisky for the officers and WOs class two,
   The solitary drink of beer that must suffice for you,
The times the 'Higher-ups' declare must be entirely free
   Until the order is received 'Reveille' HALF PAST THREE.

The tension of the waiting for an early morn attack,
   The time you spend in wondering if you ever will get back,
The awe-inspiring silence on a lonely night patrol
   When you come up to the enemy and know you've reached
                                                      your goal.

The building of the shelters with grass and stout bamboo,
   The floating clouds up in the sky so very seldom blue,
The journey to the cookhouse right up a steep incline
   With never chairs or tables set out for you to dine.

No huge parade for victory through a brick-built western town,
   Just a few old shacks and mud huts that are often falling
                                                          down,
That is the tale of the "Royals' the men who fight out here
   They win their hard-fought battles but seldom get a cheer.

I suppose it must be our luck to raise the banner high
   In the rugged mountain country away from human eye,
Small wonder we are saying in the dreary jungle spot
   That this is the British army that Britain soon forgot.

Royal Scots Fusiliers

THE INFANTEER

He was born to the earth; on the day he enlists
    He is sentenced to life on the soil,
To march on it, crawl on it, dig in it, sprawl on it,
    And sleep on it after his toil.

Be it sand, rock, or ice, gravel, mud or red loam
    He will fight on it bravely, will die,
And the crude little cross telling men of his loss,
    Will cry mutely to some foreign sky.

He's the tired looking man in the untidy garb,
    Weatherbeaten, footsore with fatigue,
But his spirit is strong as he marches along
    With his burdens, for league upon league.

He attacks in the face of a murderous fire,
    Crawling forward, attacking through mud.
When he breaks through the lines, over wire and mines,
    On the point of his bayonet is blood.

Should you meet him, untidy, begrimed and fatigued,
    Don't indulge in unwarranted mirth,
For the brave infanteer deserves more than your sneer,
    He is truly the salt of the earth.

A Gunner (NX70702)

This is reprinted from June *'Duckboard'* Magazine,
Australia.

THE BLOKE IN BURMA

You'll fail to find him mentioned in the papers every day,
   The news is all of Europe and not of Mandalay,
But away in far-off Burma, midst the sun and dust and rain,
   There's a little chap who's fighting hard, a few mud huts
                             to gain.
He doesn't fight for prizes like a city or a town,
   It's just a chaung or feature that he's adding to his crown,
And though there's no comparison in value or in space,
   The odds against the little chap are twice as hard to face.
Today one-twenty in the shade, the air is still as death,
   Tomorrow, monsoon rains so cold they take away his breath.
Fever tears his body down, but his spirit still is game,
   No one reads of what he's done, but he does it just the same.
When the war is over he'll have no awards galore,
   You may not even notice him (in the pub – sat by the door)
Whilst others boast of what they did, he'll simply smile and say
   – "I only fought in Burma, from Mogaung to Mandalay."

36th British Div. Infantryman.

ANOPHELES LAMENT

The mozzies round my net each night,
   Sing tearfully their sad refrain,
That it is easy to get in
   But once they're in they must remain.
For, as they found, their tiny 'tums'
   Soon swelled when they staked their claim
And little holes that let them in,
   Would never let them out again.

L. A. W.

111.

THE 19TH DAGGER DIVISION

They called them Indian Home Guards,
   Little knowing there'd come a day
When the 'Dagger' would prove it's 'mettle'
   On the road to Mandalay.
The Welsh, the Berks, and Worcesters,
   Johnny Gurkha: The mighty few!
The Sikh, Baluch, and Assams,
   The Royal Artillery too.
Commanded by their leader
   The 'Pocket General' Reece;
They drove the Jap from Imphal
   It's safeguard right and peace.
They fought to the Irrawaddy,
   Crossed it, on rafts of bamboo;
Captured a feature duly named 'Pear Hill'
   And so formed a 'bridgehead', at Singu.
Then over the dry and barren plains
   They trecked their southward way
Fighting a foe, who fanatically
   Contested this road to Mandalay.
But on and on went the 'Dagger Div'
   Dirty, tired, but gay,
Mandalay Hill was their great prize,
   Came the battle for Mandalay;
Fort Dufferin walls were sorely rent,
   Mitchells bombed all day,
The 'Dagger' made a final thrust –
   Ending the fight for Mandalay.
But those gallant lads who fought there
   Knew the price they'd had to pay,
In comrades who had fallen
   In the quest for Mandalay.

Written by *Two Members of 19 Div. R.E.M.E.*

DREAMS OF HOPE

To stroll with you down a country lane,
  Or weed a garden once again;
To see again English flowers, English trees
  And feel a gentle summer breeze,
To have the snow, the dew, the rain,
  And see the frost on a window pane.

To hear the distant church bells ringing,
  The lovely sound of children singing,
Or just to listen to the charms
  Of Gershwin, Schubert and Brahms.
To watch a film, to see a play,
  Or perhaps to dance the hours away.

To see the Trent in Trentham Gardens,
  Or to watch the cattle on the farms.
To drink good beer in a village pub,
  Or sip champagne in a local club,
To stay at home and hear the news,
  And listen to the speaker's views.

These are the things and many more,
  They are the things worth fighting for.

Eric Roger Tooth

The author of this poem lies buried at Trimulgherry, Secunderabad, where he died of hepatitis on 17 May 1945, whilst recovering from wounds received in Burma. He served with 1 Commando, and at the time of his death was just 19 years old.

(Thanks to Mr. A. T. Vaughan, Hon Secretary, Forest of Dean Branch)

THE REUNION

We came down to London by coach, car and train,
 The Burma Reunion is on once again,
Twelve months have gone by since the last time we met
 In the Great Albert Hall to remember, and yet,
There are some who were with us in April last year
 Who are not with us now, or their loved ones so dear.
They have gone on ahead to prepare us a place
 Where all men are comrades, whatever their race.
Some there will be meeting pals once again
 Will be absent next year, but their memories remain
To add to the others we'll see ne'er again
 We left them there, silent, on the grim Imphal Plain,
Down by the road from Kohima where hard battles were won
 By the brave men of Britain, with bayonet and gun.
Some gave of their lives in the green Arakan,
 They never gave in to the beasts from Japan.
Some were left there by the Nyakydauk Pass
 In a spot clear of Jungle, not covered in grass.
Furness and Bushell, these names I recall,
 They died not by bullet, but by bombs that did fall
From the Nippons small planes, coming in from the sun
 And out again, low, missed by our own Bofors Gun.
We lowered them gently, not encased in wood
 But wrapped in a blanket, two brave men and good
They fought and they died, but it wasn't in vain,
 Supreme was their sacrifice, honoured their name.
The years have gone by, now we sit and recall
 Comrades like these in the Great Albert Hall.
The Kohima Epitaph is spoken with care,
 Reverence too, because we were there.
The Spirit of Comradeship, nurtured in war
 Reveals itself now, as never before;
The smile that says 'welcome', the shake of a hand
 May baffle a stranger, but we understand.
For there's a bond that still binds us, great ones and small;
 At our Twenty-eighth Reunion in the Great Albert Hall.

     Dennis H. B. Millward, Ex-Sgt Royal Artillery

THE LAST RIVER

The green slow flowing river drifting by,
  Takes crossing gunners o'er its wide expanse,
Meanwhile good friends stand by their trusty guns,
  Covering the flimsy vessels slow advance.
What thoughts assail those drawing near the shore,
  Knowing full well the cruelties of war?

The wide slow flowing river drifting by,
  Perchance has beauty in an artists' eye,
Yet others, fearful of a loathsome fate,
  See nought but evil in its endless spate.
Soldiers of war, with foe on distant land,
  Must courage take from comrades close at hand.

The last slow flowing river drifting by,
  So truly last for those about to die,
Last too, for Bob to see, for screaming lead
  Took from him sight, but nothing more;
For Yorkshire's son, so long our trusty friend,
  This was to be beginning, not the end.
For we all know, all those who loved him well,
  That courage, steadfastness begat by war,
Upheld him yet, though he could see no more.

Warren Bugler,
114 (Sussex) Field Regiment
Royal Artillery (TA)

To Bob Foster, 114 (Sussex) Field Regiment, RA (TA), gallant comrade in arms, who was blinded crossing the Irrawaddy 1944. Bob came home, married Joy and, never ceasing to love his 'Regiment', was an inspiration to all in his family, church and business.

THEIR REMEMBRANCE

Where do all these men come from?
    The small child asked his mum,
I saw them here last year as well,
    Why do they all come?
They come, she said, to pay respect
    To comrades that they lost,
Who fought to give us freedom,
    For which many paid the cost.
These men still remember
    When they fought there afar,
And that is why they wear today
    A shining 'Burma Star'.
They were the 'Forgotten Army',
    But we never should forget
The dreadful things they suffered,
    And some still suffer yet.
So remember all these men son,
    When you kneel and pray,
It's because of what they then endured
    That we are free today.

Written by **Mrs Doris Moore**
of Stowmarket

TOGETHERNESS

Oh, leave me not when far away,
    But let your thoughts abide,
That I may find you every day,
    Unseen yet by my side.

I could not bear to leave you thus,
    Unless this thought be true,
That parting cannot sever us
    And I am still with you.

Your voice I hear when others speak,
    Though none will ever guess,
And yours the presence I shall seek
    In all my loneliness.

Be this the comfort of the night,
    The blessing of the day
Your love and nearness be my light
    While we are far away.

Anonymous

Sent by a 'Friend' from Reading, having received this from a soldier who was wounded at Dunkirk and later killed in action 'out East'.

DOWN BY MANDALAY

Out there in the jungle, down by Mandalay,
    A few forgotten soldiers slowly fight their way,
They dream of the girls they left back home,
    And soon they hope to cross the foam
To see their land and loved ones,
    Never more to roam.

Some of them are repat, some are time expired,
    Longing for their troopship and their fireside.
They often talk of Burmese plains
    Of dust and heat and monsoon rains,
Of roads that lead to heaven
    And tracks that lead to hell.

Now all you lads from Blighty, who travel far from home,
    Who never liked the cities of Tripoli and Rome,
Remember the lads who fought and dwelt
    In jungles green where brasses melt
And Japs were more like monkeys
    And mozzies bites were felt.

Now when this war is over and the job is done
    All you lads from Burma go tell it to your son;
Remember the war against the Hun
    But don't forget the war we won
In Asia's South-East corner,
    Against the Rising Sun.

Author not known

(This can be sung to the tune of Lilli Marlene)

118.

THE UNEXPECTED PORT OF CALL

A cry was heard, "Chaps! There's land ahead!",
  And we all tumbled out of bed;
Up the stairs and on the deck
  To see the shore, with outstretched neck,
A pale blue sea and golden sand,
  With whitened soil, as you looked inland,
Topped with palm trees green and bright,
  Which made a truely lovely sight.

We watched awhile, then came the crave
  To breakfast, wash and shave,
Lay out our kit and blankets fold,
  So made our way back down to the hold,
Then when our morning task was done
  We raced upstairs in to the sun,
And once more on deck and sitting down,
  There on our right we saw a town.

Beloved buildings great and small
  Mingled with the palm-trees tall;
Steeples and towers rose on high
  With birds flying in the sky.
Then we pulled into the dock,
  And bells were chiming eight-o-clock;
Buildings here were vast and few
  And blocked out most of our view.

Rails and Lifeboats, crammed with troops,
  Stared at the natives, stood in groups,
Yelling, shouting, going mad,
  Throwing down the coins they had;
Police and firemen down below,
  Started dashing to and fro,
Then someone in a khaki suit,
  Yelled to a native for some fruit.

Pineapples were the boys delight,
  And eyes aglow at such a sight,
To see them in their birthday skin
  Not just chopped up and in a tin;
Then looking some way from the rail
  They found a great big dirty pail,
A bob a time, the price agreed,
  They lowered the bucket for their need.

After dinner someone said,
  "We are going ashore" – boy did it spread,
Down the stairs we almost flew
  For shorts and hose-tops too,
Washing, shaving, running here and there,
  Boots and socks were everywhere,
Sweating streams and feeling wrecks,
  We staggered once more to the decks.

Lined up, roll call, about turn,
  We marched away down from the stern,
And on the quayside down below,
  We lined up for the word to go,
Left right left right and away,
  We left the ship for our short stay;
Through the gates and up the hill
  In perfect order and goodwill.

People flocked into the street
  To hear the band and marching feet,
Black and white, fat and thin,
  They all came out to hear the din,
Laughing and staring at the sight,
  Waving hands with all their might,
Then up the hill, which slowly passed
  And into the town we proudly marched.

Trees grew all along the street,
   And people walking in bare feet,
Trams and lorries stopped and stayed,
   While people from their windows swayed,
March to attention came the shout,
   Swing 'em up and not about,
Then came the moment of the day,
   "Eyes right! – you – look this way."

On we marched with all eyes right,
   People stared at such a sight,
Beating drums and bugles blew,
   Then the CO came into view,
Eye to eye, we plodded past
   Till it came to "Eyes front!" at last,
"Right wheel, get 'em up," the shout,
   "Left, right! Halt! One two! Fall out!"

"Don't go away," the next cry came,
   "Just stick around." – Gee what a shame,
Still 'twas nice being on dry land again,
   So we just wandered round in vain,
Then in our midst from the unknown
   A great bald fruit was thrown,
"Pass it up," came a deep voiced cry
   And through the air it whistled by.

Tired out the game soon stopped,
   And on the scene some negroes popped.
Now for some fun the boys all cried
   To see the negroes look pop-eyed,
Questions asked and signs shown,
   But, having a language of their own,
We gave it up as a bad job,
   And amused ourselves with the coloured mob.

121.

There were hundreds strolling up and down,
  Men and women, black and brown,
We laughed at them, they laughed at us,
  And the girls giggled and made a fuss,
Then slowly as the sun went down
  The lights blazed up all over town,
Windows, spires, cone-shaped towers
  Blazed just like a bowl of flowers.

Some bugle notes then rent the air,
  "Fall in," they said – it wasn't fair,
To march us back aboard the ship,
  There's hours yet, before we 'kip':
But there it was, we had to go
  And being soldiers dare not say no,
Then lining up into threes,
  We waited at the 'stand at ease'.

The order came and turning right
  We marched on through the coloured light,
Hundreds lined the way each side,
  On pavements, roads, so thick and wide,
Cheering, shouting, in their glee
  With their fingers formed a 'V',
Girls all ogled with their eyes,
  And in their language said goodbye.

Then came the ship into sight,
  All ablaze with electric light,
Through the gate and on the quay,
  And longing for a cup of tea.
Once aboard and in the hold
  We queued for tea, good as gold,
Tea was good, so out we went,
  Happy, full up, and content.

On top-deck in the open air
  We smoked away without a care,
No blackout to think of and fear
  In this strange place, so far, so near,
And this we did 'til half past ten,
  Then back down to the sleeping den,
And there we lay in slumber deep,
  'til someone yelled out in their sleep.

Then so much for our trip ashore
  And back aboard the ship once more
We lean against the rail and see
  This lovely land against the sea.
Shore leave stopped, and in the bay,
  We, with patience, await the day
When early in the morning say:
  "Sailor! Is this our port for another short stay?"

Tom Webber

The foregoing piece was written in 1942 by Tom Webber, Ex-Sgt of the Medical Section of the 9th Batt., The Royal Sussex Regiment. The battalion, together with the 6th SWBs, and 10th Gloucesters were in transit to India aboard the Athlone Castle and the Stirling Castle, when, due to the massive presence of 'U' boats off the west coast of Africa, they were diverted to the neutral port of Bahia in Brazil. This convoy of two troopers, plus one escort, is believed to be the only one ever to call at this port during the war.

The importance of this march, through the town of Bahia, was that the day we called was the Brazilian National Day, and the Senior Officer with the ships was asked if we could honour them with a parade through the town.

To the Burma Soldier

You seldom hit the headlines,
And you never make a fuss,
But you fight the Japs in Burma
Just to help the likes of us.

In the forest swamps and jungle,
In a climate far from kind,
You dream of England – Home –
And the folks you left behind.

Now the Japs are dirty fighters
And you have to get them quick,
As he waits for you in the treetops
Like a monkey up a stick.

So I salute the Fourteenth Army,
Who are ready for the days
When they've hurled the Japs from Burma,
To them it's home sweet home again.

Mrs E Poulton,
Northampton
Written in 1944

'To all our Fighting Soldiers – God Bless you All'

HE DIED IN BURMA IN 1944

He died, this soldier buried by the track,
  Not in the fever of some great attack,
Not for the grand objective, nor the high
  Gains that the jingo headlines cry.

He died, without the knowledge in his heart
  That dying, he would play some little part
In writing 'Finish' to a bloody tale
  Seeing the dawn as he went down the vale.

He died to gain no more than just a mound,
  Unknown, un-mapped – a yard or so of ground;
To be abandoned when the monsoon came.

He died, the touch of English breezes cold,
Cold on his cheek and in his heart grown old.
He died, the savour of good English earth,
  Faint in the fragrance, distant in its mirth.

You earth that shrouds him now in this strange
                         place,
  Lie gently, as if English, on his face.

Written in Burma
Author not known.

A TRIBUTE TO THOSE OF KOHIMA

In the heat and through monsoon,
    They could pay the piper's tune,
For their courage was unequalled, even there!
    Where the Chindits went before,
These men added to their score,
    And they won a battle honour with great flair –
Kohima was it's name, and they earned undying fame,
    In the jungles and the deserts, as of yore,
Now, as years roll by, our pride,
    Is with those who fought and died,
In their efforts to stem the tide of war.

The FAITHFULS paid the price,
    In the land of teak and rice,
They made their mark, for all the world to see,
    In the Glory of their Dead,
They battled on ahead,
    Played a part out east, to set all Nations free.

John Allan
Ex-D L I.

126.

THE ROAD TO MANDALAY

Rangoon – and the peaceful palm trees and spicy eastern smells
And the golden domed pagoda with it's sleepless wind-rocked
bells,
The Yellow Scourge swept over it one sad and fateful day
And sent us scurrying north-ward on the road to Mandalay.

The god-descended warriors – we could hear them at our backs
As we squelched through oozy-paddy fields and labyrinthine
tracks,
Through nullahs and through jungles where tortuous creepers
twined
And every thorn and towering tree had crouching death behind.

Malaria, snakes, mosquitoes, crawling Japs and stifling heat,
And thinning ranks still fighting through a thousand mile
retreat!
Oh! England was an opium dream a thousand miles away
As we crossed the Indian frontier on our trek from Mandalay.

But we fought the Japs and held them and we're thrashing
them with rods,
And the god-descended warriors look anything but gods!
For now we're trekking southwards and the yellow men turn
grey
As they ponder Hari-Kiri on the road to Mandalay.

The peacock on his field of gold – claws down the rising sun,
And vengence trails the little men however fast they run,
For we left our dead behind us, there's a mighty debt to pay
Now we're rolling back like thunder – on the road to Mandalay.

C. A. Renshaw, (A New Zealander)

127.

To My Friends
– Chunkai POW Camp, Thailand, 1944

Once more there dawns another Christmas morn,
    Once more the passing of another year
Brings home to us, who often are forlorn,
    The sense of passing time, of bondage drear.
We live for hope, and all too oft' it seems
    A hollow mockery, a sordid jest
To men who have so little but their dreams
    To ease the pang of hearts and minds oppress'd.
Who knows what life will hold, or changeful fate,
    For us who wait and watch and hope and pray?
We know this only, whatsoe'er our state
    We have our friends whom none can take away.
First comes our God; the dearest and the best
    We name Him, Saviour, King and Lord;
Nor scorn the earthly friends whom loves attest
    The fellowship his promises afford.
They only smooth the steep, the rugged way,
    Make bearable the all too heavy load,
Give solace through the hot and weary day,
    And cheer the gloom that ere our hearts bestrode.
To them let thanks be given this Christmas Day,
    To God our Saviour, born this time on earth,
And to our comrades may we ever pray
    A happier future stayed in that dear birth.

This poem was sent to Miss Elizabeth Burns, S. S. Chitral, in the Red Sea, Sunday 14 October 1945, with best wishes from **John Roach**.

THE MOZZIE

Thou wretched plague, thou saboteur, thou pest,
  Thou vile infester of each stagnant place,
Thou ruthless interferer of my rest,
  Thou savage biter of my hands and face,
Thou trespasser within my sacred net.
  Thou rude disturber of my peaceful dream,
I'll be avenged of thee, I'll get thee yet,
  To arms! To legs! Apply the mozzie cream.

Frolic

UNFORGOTTEN ARMY
(The Mawchi Road)

The rain-drenched cloak of darkness wetly falls
  And fills the night with silent chilling dread;
No stars or moon to light the endless void,
  For we who saw the dawn and now are dead.

Our weary steps had spanned an endless day,
  From broken bridge to crumbling spade-hewn cell;
The ringing in our deafened ears for e'er,
  The splitting whiplash of a random shell.

And now crouched low in sunken sodden pits,
  We soundless cling to all-embracing loam;
The jungle silence brooks no requiem
  For we who died so very far from home.

Only memory now holds back the door
  Before we drift and fade beyond recall
Remember us for what we were and gave,
  Our hopes, our dreams, our love of life – our all.

Gordon Nimse

129.

A Tribute to Lord Louis Mountbatten

Feel proud to say 'I knew him'
    At the mention of his name,
Or be less proud to shed a tear
    For grief exceeds all pain.

In war and peace we owed him much,
    For none could take his place,
Our thanks to him who led the way
    And made our journey safe.

And while the world, in silent grief,
    Pays tribute to his name,
Remember those who shared his fate
    And those who bear the pain.

A Sailor, Soldier, Diplomat –
    An example to all men.
Unlikely we shall ever see
    The likes of him again.

From ***A Burma Star veteran***

Women of the Rose

There's a Place in Heaven for Harlots,
    And that the Soldier knows.
There's a thousand-and-one with a heart of gold,
    Who wear the shameful Rose.
When a man turns his back on the trenches. . .
    (Where 'Home' means ten-thousand miles)
From the filth and the soul-searing hell that is War;
    He's starved, for a wise woman's smiles.

Only she, of the Oldest Profession,
    With her nylons and sweet-scented breath
Can untangle the nerves, and comfort the minds
    Of men who have tangled with Death!
'Twas Fate that played her the joker
    And made her an object of scorn. . .
You Ladies of Virtue, who know not of lust,
    Thank God for the day you were born.
You may cry out in shocked indignation,
    But know you that my words are true,
That Jesus of Nazareth died on His Cross
    For the Harlots, the same as for you.

Ian E. Kaye

The Fourteenth Army

They have gone past, men of the shield and sword,
    Last of our fame, and half a world away
From all familiar things; so let them rest
    Now that the battle's done. The jungle way,
From Naga Hill and over Chindwin's banks,
    Will hear no more their green-limbed stealthy tread,
Or watch with fevered eyes where tanks have gone,
    And little boats, and where a man lies dead.
Across their airlines blow the purple clouds,
    Water and grass and nameless twilight things
Press after them, and cover close their tracks,
    And where their voices whispered, silence clings.
An army passes, but its love remain,
    Freedom – and a way home through the jungle rain.

Lockhart Howell

131.

The Birth of The Burma Star

O mother earth! Once more the bugles called
    So many of your young sons to fight another war,
Their destinies they knew not where
    But for the sounds of Freedom they were to care,
The day of yesterday found them in jungle green
    A Forgotten Army – heard of but rarely seen.

The battle was fought, and won the sinking of
                    the cruel sun,
    And you mother earth chose those sons to keep
Close to your breast, forever in blessed sleep.
    Back from the jungles their comrades came
Older and wiser – for the young ones remain –
    But with them they brought an awakening Light,
A Star of Friendship, Which Heart and Hands unite –
    Their Star of Tomorrow – Today – and Tonight.

        The Burma Star was born.

                      Edna May Ferraro,
                      1978 (Pinwe Club)

On Belatedly Joining the Association

No one who was not there
   Can appreciate the atmosphere
Of that room.
   The firm handshake and the smile
To dispel one's gloom.
There were no badges of rank,
   No stripe, no pip,
No crown.
   But every man a man of valour,
Of stature and renown.

Travel the whole world over,
   Search near and far,
Never will you find a finer crowd
   Than the men of the Burma Star.

Anonymous

Memories of Pinwe

Memories of those Burma days, my friends,
   Yes, memories ring clear, of how one Sunday,
T'was the tenth day of November '44,
   When we the Royal Sussex for Pinwe set forth
Along the railway, to the South,
   Through jungle dense and green,
Hiding an enemy, entrenched in foxholes 'neath the trees,
   So cunningly deployed, so deadly and unseen.

Yes, memories still clear dear friends,
    Of an eerie silence broken
By the harsh realities of battle.
    Yes, the staccato sound of the Jap Whizz-bang,
And their distinctive machine gun rattle,
    Their resistance stubborn and strong,
And our coolness and our mettle,
    Yes, and our discipline unshaken.

More memories to mind my friends,
    Of the fourth day of the battle;
The Nips fanatical charge at everything in sight,
    Their orders complete, no regard for life;
The Emperor's Guard had picked a fight,
    How we responded with all our might,
And picked them off. Oh! What a sight!
    We men from the 'Sussex' seasoned warriors all,
Resisted, fought hard and sat tight,
    No time to think of blighty or the wife.

The memory of that day dear friends,
    And the cost of the battle,
The comrades lost, and those wounded, their pain,
    We remember them all, everyone a friend;
Our servants the Mules who had given their best,
    Wounded in battle, we laid them to rest.
The Jap dead, three score, may've been more,
    They paid the price, for us the gain.
The ammo, the rations and rum for the taking,
    Our stores replenished, for us the next battle.

Yes, more memories dear friends
    Of the battle for the 'chaungs',
With the fighting tough and bitter,
    The cost and the strain remembered;
Nothing conceded, but, oh! the struggle,
    T'was desperate and cruel, what a battle;
Yes, Pinwe proved hard to conquer,
    We gave our best, some gave their all.

134.

We remember also my friends,
    The battle of the 'Guns',
At dusk the Chinese Mortars, bombarding –
    And reverberating, through the jungle runs;
What a racket! What a shindy! Yes, quite fright'ning,
    Blasting the devil out of Jap,
Who had the choice, we wished them well
    On their way to their ancestors or hell.

Much more we remember dear friends,
    The stillness and the tremoring
Of an earthquake somewhere near,
    Of the Padre and his services
In the jungle far from home;
    The jungle cocks a crowing,
Before the crack of dawn,
    The Dakotas and their airdrops of everything
For us, sometimes forgotten, mail from home;
    Yes! We remember them clear.

Lastly dear friends, we remember
    Of how we battled on, for sixteen days, not fun,
Time had no meaning, a job to be done;
    Pinwe eluded us, not our prize to win,
For us a respite from battle, our task complete.
    We moved out and moved on
To Katha, for Christmas and thence on;
    'Twas 29 Brigade who walked in,
Not a Jap in sight, they had gone,
    But, for us the knowledge, ours was a job well done.

                  (Sandy) H. E. Williams, Ex-Sgt
                  9th Royal Sussex Regt.

To The Memory of My Pal

He slept so peacefully on that hot February night,
  When suddenly, the Japs attacked us – over on our right.
He woke up quickly, thinking this was some prank,
  It was then the bullet caught him, and he rolled down
Early next morning the sad report came back,   [the bank.
  He had died looking up to heaven,
With a bullet in his back.
  He died so young, he died so brave,
Only his loved ones know what he gave.
  He went without warning, he went without fear,
To you he was no one – to me he was dear.
  He made life so human, he made life so sweet,
No more shall I hear the steps of his feet.
  He went without malice, he went with a smile,
He now rests in Heaven, a rest that's worthwhile.
  When the war is over and victory is ours
I'll go to his grave and there lay my flowers.
  To that dusty desolate country,
Where there isn't any fun,
  Beneath the shady bamboo, and the Red Hot Burma Sun.

So now you know the story
  Of my pal so young and brave,
Of how he went to glory, and the cause for which he gave,
  He now lies blazed in glory, in the land across the wave,
The comrades who saw and knew him
  And live today that tell, of my great pal Arnold,
And the cause for which he fell.
  Some day later on I'll meet him
Somewhere, way up there,
  And I'll tell him how I missed him
And we'll both kneel in prayer.

P. Tabron, Conway Branch

136.

Xmas 1989

Old comrades mine, we celebrate
    We are alive today
The Good Lord chose a kindly fate
    To lead us on our way.

Nigh on fifty years we joined our 'mob'
    And answered "Country's call",
We left our kinsfolk, home and job
    To face what might befall.

We had our comrades, brave and strong,
    Who fought by us through Hell,
They gave us courage, comfort, long
    Like brothers, till they fell.

Alas, in jungle, paddy field and seas
    Farewell to loving arms and home,
To give us lucky ones a spell of peace.
    A debt to them we owe!

This Xmas, as we all regale,
    Remember those, as life extends
And raise a glass 'To Absent Pals'
    And 'mother, wife and friends'!

Joe Oliver
Ex-11th (East Africans) Div
Arakan, Burma.

THE FORESTER'S FAREWELL TO HIROHITO

We 'ave heard of that kerfuffle,
 Of that bloke in far Japan,
Who went to that there funeral
 To plant that wicked man.
We 'ave heard of all the shouting,
 – Blokes yelling at the prince –
But 'im, like us, just done 'is job,
 No matter what they thinks.

We still think that 'is soldiers
 Were a lot of heathen tykes.
We don't want resignations –
 Or one man hunger strikes.
We know we're getting ancient,
 Old fighters of the jungle,
What's done is done, we can't forget
 – 'Old memories', we mumble.

We faced you, Son of Heaven,
 Faced with death, disease, mosquito,
We blotted out your sunshine then,
 We squashed you, Hirohito.

 Ron Day
  CHAIRMAN, 1955-1981,
  Burma Star Association,
  Forest of Dean Branch

INDEX OF FIRST LINES

INDEX OF FIRST LINES

Our principal fields of publication are not normally concerned either with poetry nor with military matters. We do not in general publish fiction. Whilst we are willing occasionally to consider manuscripts outside our normal fields it is **always** desirable to send a preliminary letter and we cannot, at present, encourage the submission of manuscripts other than those dealing with matters of particular Lincolnshire interest.

We do have two books in print which, in addition to being of interest to the local area, are of considerable interest to many involved in the 1939 – '45 war.

CRIMSON SKIES by *Charlie Framp*

THE HISTORY OF A TWENTIETH CENTURY ENGLISH WORKING MAN

Pp. 284   0 902662 83 X Paperback edn.   £5.25

0 902662 82 1 Cased edn.   £12.50

This is the story of a boy growing up in the thirties and joining the army, as so many did then, at the age of eighteen. His war was spent mainly in North Africa and the advance through Italy, including a hair-raising involvement in the Monte Casino siege. According to the author he was a 'born private'. Wounded on more than one occasion, after the war he became a bricklayer in the Scunthorpe steelworks and, almost by accident, a shop steward. His account of the steelworks from the working man's point of view is both interesting and revealing.

In a Foreward to this book Lord (Len) Murray writes:

" ... *I have never read a more gripping account of the war as experienced by a private soldier. ... We are all in debt to this English infantryman and shop steward both for what he did and for his account of it.*"

Details of our other Life in Lincolnshire titles are available on request. They can be purchased through any good bookseller or can often be obtained through the Library Service.

Boston at War is No XII in a series we publish concerned with the local history of Boston (Lincolnshire).

BOSTON AT WAR by *Martin Middlebrook*

Pp. 88   0 902662 62 7 saddlestitched   £1.50

This is a fascinating account of the involvement of a small country market town in the wars of this century. Although primarily of interest to those interested in Boston it is written by a man who has, since the time he wrote this small booklet, become internationally known as a modern war historian.

Martin Middlebrook's first book **The First Day on the Somme** was inspired by a visit to the 1914 – '18 battlefields in the 1960s and his realisation that, unless action was taken quickly, the recollections of men actually involved would soon be lost for ever. The book was so successful that he has gone on from strength to strength using particularly the technique of personal statements from people actually involved combined with an historical overview of the events of the time.

So far Martin Middlebrook's books have been concerned mainly with the European and Atlantic theatres of war (OPERATION CORPORATE and THE FIGHT FOR THE MALVINAS are two recent books and are concerned with the Falklands war).

The one book dealing with some aspect of the Japanese war is:

BATTLESHIP *Martin Middlebrook and Patrick Mahoney*

Malaya, December 1941, the sinking of *HMS Prince of Wales* and *HMS Repulse.*

These two ships were sent by Churchill to deter Japan from entering the war. Through a series of mishaps and mistakes they were caught at sea, without air cover, and both were sunk by Japanese aircraft with the loss of 840 lives. The blow to British prestige and power in the Far East was catastrophic. This book describes the dispatch of the ships to Singapore and their subsequent fate, through meticulous research and then through the eyes of the survivors. The book is called **Battleship** because, in the opinion of the authors, this incident marks the end of the 'battleship era'.   0 14 004899 5 – Penguin paperback   £5.99

All Martin Middlebrook's major books are published under the Allen Lane/Penguin imprint from whom details are available.